MW01110184

Legal Whores

Legal Whores

© Copyright 2002 Thomas A. Binford. All rights reserved.

No part of this publication may be reproduced, stored in a retrieval system, or transmitted, in any form or by any means, electronic, mechanical, photocopying, recording, or otherwise, without the written prior permission of the author.

Printed in Victoria, Canada

National Library of Canada Cataloguing in Publication Data

Binford, Thomas A., 1938-
  Legal whores / Thomas A. Binford.
Includes bibliographical references.
ISBN 1-55369-672-7
  1. Practice of law--United States--Corrupt practices. I. Title.
KF300.Z9B56 2002   364.16'8   C2002-902914-7

TRAFFORD

This book was published _on-demand_ in cooperation with Trafford Publishing.
On-demand publishing is a unique process and service of making a book available for retail sale to the public taking advantage of on-demand manufacturing and Internet marketing.
On-demand publishing includes promotions, retail sales, manufacturing, order fulfilment, accounting and collecting royalties on behalf of the author.

Suite 6E, 2333 Government St., Victoria, B.C. V8T 4P4, CANADA

Phone	250-383-6864	Toll-free	1-888-232-4444 (Canada & US)
Fax	250-383-6804	E-mail	sales@trafford.com
Web site	www.trafford.com	TRAFFORD PUBLISHING IS A DIVISION OF TRAFFORD HOLDINGS LTD.
Trafford Catalogue #02-0485		www.trafford.com/robots/02-0485.html

10   9   8   7   6   5

Table of Contents

DISCLAIMER...Nothing in this book is to be construed as legal advice; all are the opinions of the author. For legal advice seek the services of a competent attorney.

DEDICATION

This primer is dedicated to the poor, ignorant masses that won't read it. Former President Clinton refers to them as "Joe Six Pack". They are the approximate 60 million individuals who can't afford the services of an attorney. They are called PRO SE LITIGANTS. They represent themselves in the judicial system. Historically, Pro Se Litigants in this country have been brutally raped and pillaged financially by the judicial system. They have found the judicial system in this country not unlike a giant cancer that continues to spread, eating any and all normal and productive cells in its path.

The typical Pro Se Litigant will not read this primer. You may wonder, then, why I am writing it. I am writing this book for myself. It is something I feel obligated to do. Nevertheless, let's have some fun and continue...

Legal Whores

13PREAMBLE

Being a relatively successful businessman in my early sixties, I have seen a lot of commendable events and likewise a great deal of skullduggery in the business world. The preponderance of these events are usually born out of the quest for money. I have found that in no other vocation does the hunger for money supersede any and all other values like it does in the legal or judicial fields. I must qualify these remarks by saying that I am referring to "lawyers and judges". Occasionally the feeling or exercise of power syndrome either by itself or jointly with the thirst for money also precludes other values. Let me define these so-called other values to which I refer as being God, family, honesty, fairness, integrity, and truthfulness, among others. There is nothing wrong with the word profit if one does not preclude all other values to attain this goal.

"The number of people serving as their own attorneys is soaring --- to the dismay of many in the state court system."[1] In 65% of the divorce cases filed in Florida, at least one of the parties doesn't have a lawyer. As stated in my dedication, there are literally tens of millions of folks in these United States in need of affordable legal assistance yet unable to find it. That fact struck me about nine years ago, and I decided to do something about it. I attended a HALT convention in Atlanta in 1991. This is a national group dedicated to improving access to the courts in this country for Pro Se Litigants (those representing themselves in legal matters). At this convention I met a fellow by the name of Alfred Adask who had just started publishing a periodical called THE ANTISHYSTER. I must admit, Mr. Adask and his periodical really got my attention. Apparently, Mr. Adask, a roofer by trade, lost his children, lost his meager assets and got railroaded by the Texas judicial system in his divorce. He was financially and emotionally devastated. From that point on, Alfred Adask has dedicated his life to exposing the (Texas) judicial system for what it really is. In fact, each issue of his Antishyster magazine contains an advertisement offering

---

[1] Orlando Sentinel 7/23/2000

$10,000.00 in cash for any person that can produce for him an honest lawyer in the State of Texas. To date, no one has collected. Mr. Adask is not my role model by any means but he did have an influence on me pursuing this endeavor.

For purposes of explanation let me define the term independent paralegals. Sometimes they are also referred to as legal technicians. Independent paralegals are persons that do not work under the supervision of an attorney. They produce a myriad of legal documents in addition to research. Their work product goes to attorneys as well as to the public. They cannot represent anyone in a court of law. Their work product, which goes to the general public and is thereby circumventing the lawyer's fees, tends to be scrutinized very closely by the state Bar associations under so-called unlicensed practice of law statutes.

Subsequent to attending the HALT convention and reading a myriad of propaganda put out by the State Bar and the American Bar Associations, I set out to visit any independent paralegals that I could find in my state. My intent was to find out (1) were there any practicing independent paralegals, and (2) would they confide in me as to what they were really doing? These free lance paralegals did not know me and could easily assume that I was a part of a series of sting operations for the Florida Bar. The Bar has been known to stoop to such efforts. I could not blame them if these paralegals were recalcitrant to my efforts to communicate with them. You see, the legal fraternity loves to intimidate (potential) independent paralegals with the Unlicensed Practice of Law (UPL) Florida Statute violation charge. This law simply states that one who is not a member of the Florida Bar can not practice law in the State of Florida. If you do so, you are guilty of violating UPL. This law is not unique in Florida and holds true in virtually every state of the Union. The definition of UPL to the legal fraternity is whatever the Bar wants it to be. For example, if I were to give you my opinion of the Florida Constitution, technically I would be practicing law, violating the unlicensed practice of law statute. Anyway, the reception I received was overwhelmingly in my favor. Most of the independent paralegals with whom I met were in business less than a year, and the Florida Bar and local attorneys were beating on them to close down. Shortly thereafter, some did go out of business. The attrition rate for independent paralegals throughout the United States is overwhelming.

Let me take a moment here and explain to the naive of you that don't understand why the legal fraternity is opposed to independent paralegals. They will tell you that the potential for serious public harm is great when an independent paralegal handles any type of legal work for you. This is unmitigated bullshit...and they know it! There are rare cases which they will cite where an independent paralegal might have caused harm to an individual in an actual case of the unlicensed practice of law. However, historically the ratio of complaints from clients against lawyers and independent paralegals runs about 500 to 1 against lawyers. In fact, the most recent statistics generated by the Bar which we were able to view, showed that ALL of the complaints filed that year against independent paralegals were filed by attorneys and not by paralegal's clients. When a qualified independent paralegal properly fills out all of the necessary documents for a simplified, non-contested dissolution of marriage with no minor children and charges $150 and the final judgment is granted in 4 to 6 weeks while an attorney quotes $5,000 and 4 to 6 months to the same couple for the same end results, where is the public harm? I'll tell you. The harm is the attorney not being able to rape this couple for $5,000+. This particular scenario is true (and common) because I personally handled it and know the attorney in question. Incidentally, it has gotten so bad that certain personnel in the Seminole County Bar Association have told me about one local attorney that averages two complaints a month from clients for over-charging. Even the Florida attorney's own periodicals, The Florida Bar News and The Florida Bar Journal, display letters to the Editor that express great disdain for the legal practice of lawyers. This book contains a variety of these letters. For example, The Florida Bar News[2] quotes a Jack T. Edmund saying, "I've been a lawyer in Florida for over 46 years, and I see over and over again why attorneys continue to blacken their own eyes. There once was a time when being a lawyer had something to do with justice. No more, it seems."

---

[2] 8/1/01

Yes, there are incompetent independent paralegals. And the Bar Association salivates at this prospect. The Bar Association loves to take such examples out of context and infer to the public that the vast majority of independent paralegals are incompetent and causing great harm to the public. Shortly after the HALT convention in Atlanta and my surrey around the state discussing this whole legal mess with various independent paralegals, we formed a state-wide independent paralegal group and petitioned the Florida Supreme Court for certification of independent paralegals. Our criteria to be a certified independent paralegal in this petition were so stringent that I don't believe half of the attorneys in Florida could have passed. As anticipated, the Florida Supreme Court denied our petition. They did not want to sanction any possible competition for their attorney brethren. Our intent is not to put attorneys out of business. That is a ludicrous assumption. There is a place and a need for competent attorneys. But there is a proven economic need for a qualified group of folks such as independent paralegals to handle many everyday mundane legal issues for the public at large including but not limited to simplified, non-contested divorces, uncontested residential evictions, simple wills, powers-of-attorney, quit claim deeds, modifications of child support, alimony and visitation matters, incorporations, and simple Chapter 7 personal bankruptcies. The fact remains that today anyone can call themselves an independent paralegal and remain in business if they can stand the heat from the Bar Association and local attorneys.

For your information, there have been several noteworthy recent trials on UPL against independent paralegals in this country. Most notably, in the Florida panhandle, two judges in different cases found the Florida UPL statute unconstitutionally vague. These county judges made a gutsy move in their respective rulings. The paralegals won round one but, of course, the Florida Bar has appealed to the Florida Supreme Court. Care to venture a guess as to how the Florida Supreme Court is going to rule? This same scenario is being repeated throughout the United States with the same dead end results...overturned by the various State Supreme Courts.

Independent paralegals should not be permitted to physically represent clients in court. This status should be reserved for competent attorneys. The legal fraternity say that independent paralegals should not aid a Pro Se Litigant who is in an adversarial posture in a legal action. Even if the Pro Se Litigant cannot afford to hire a lawyer and the other side has legal counsel representing them, tough luck. They contend that it is better to be led to the legal guillotine like a lamb to the slaughter rather than to enter the court room with substantial supporting documentation and case law, prepared by an independent paralegal, which just might help you win your case. The legal fraternity's philosophy is, pay your dues to the legal fraternity for a possible shot at victory in the court room or roll over and play dead regardless of the consequences.

My intent is to give you an idea of what to expect should you decide to represent yourself in a court room, either as the defendant or the plaintiff. The specifics which I will detail refer to Florida courts but the gist and basics should be applicable in any court in the United States. I would advise spending some time in your respective county law library prior to any such action on your part if you really go it alone without the aid of a paralegal. The judiciary is renown for periodically altering the rules of procedure in an effort to confuse Pro Se Litigants and enhance lawyer's voluminous paperwork product and subsequent fees. I am going to discuss situations involving the most common aspects of law which might involve your approach as a Pro Se Litigant. These include marital and family law, residential evictions, probate, small claims, bankruptcy, attorney fees, and the rules of civil procedure. Also, I will include a short session on appealing the lower court's ruling to the next higher court which in Florida is the District Court of Appeals. I will tell of actual occurrences regarding Pro Se Litigants, attorneys and judges. I will give you an insight into the legal profession in general. The beginnings of some chapters might mire you down in the form preparation stage but I would advise you to read on as some tasty true experiences follow. Some of my comments will definitely provide you with topics for discussion at the dinner table. Enjoy...

Legal Whores

INTRODUCTION

This book is a synopsis of the legal industry and a limited, basic "how to" for the individual that can not afford an attorney. The "how to" advice is directed to the more mundane everyday type litigation which might confront a person on a daily basis. The forms and advice might vary a little with the specific jurisdiction and the timely publishing of this manuel but the premise and foundation remain the same.

As a whole, attorneys, lawyers, judges or whatever you might call them, are known by the connotation of **LEGAL WHORES** in this non-fiction book. It is a deservedly appropriate title for this vocation. Before proceeding, please be advised that these are real, non-fiction accounts of what the legal fraternity does to extract money from the public which you might find incredible. There literally are no limits or bounds as to what the judicial fraternity will do to acquire wealth in whatever form, personal or real property. Two of the main attributes a lawyer uses to extract money from his client are the client's greed and/or emotions. The lawyer tells his client that they will win the case, and the client will probably get a zillion dollars. The typical person in these United States, being a worshipper of riches, salivates at the prospect of getting unearned moneys from the sweat of someone else. This is easy prey for the attorney.

Then there is the emotional scenario where the client is involved in a situation that incurs his emotional wrath in say marital law and its ancillary causes or confrontational issues involving neighbors, family, business. This too is easy prey for the attorney. The attorney convinces his client that he can get the best of the opposition in court, therefore, let's get'em! Whether the merits of the case warrant litigation or not is purely incidental to the attorney's desire to line his pockets with the client's cash. Most litigation is simple, requiring little cost to the litigant for resolution via mediation, arbitration or limited litigation. However, this sort of resolution puts little money in the pockets of the legal fraternity. Use psychology and prey on the client's greed and/or emotional behavioral attributes to extract the maximum amount of money (fees) from the client for the attorney's efforts...efforts as defined by the attorney. When the case or litigation is concluded the attorney no longer can bill his client for fees. Where is the incentive for the lawyer to bring this litigation to a conclusion?

`I have heard that every civilized society must have laws in order to survive. I cannot argue with this point. Nevertheless, I have great empathy with the manner in which these laws are augmented in today's society. The basic criteria for our legal system in this country is money. If you don't believe that, then you are either naive, dumb or stupid or your child is a lawyer...or all of the above. As I wrote this book there was a great divide in this country in the presidential race. The election was so close that it appeared to hinge on a few votes in Palm Beach County, Florida. The legal fraternity, minority groups and liberals have unleashed thousands of lawyers to Florida from around the country in an effort to sway the outcome to Mr. Gore. And the bottom line was money. If anyone truly believes that this scenario was about "the right to vote" or "exercising my rights" or whatever, they are very naive. I remember when Bill Clinton got elected President of the United States: the president of the Bar Association stated that Clinton's election assured additional "billions of dollars" for the coffers of the country's lawyers in various forms.[3] Had Bush Senior defeated Clinton, this would not have been the case. The lawyers, minorities, liberal organizations and similar entities fought for the election of Gore because it would have literally meant billions of dollars for them in the form of fees, judgment awards and free government handouts over at least the next four years if Gore had won the presidency. This wasn't gonna happen if George Bush became president. So you see, it's the money, not the principal. The main reason Gore got as many votes as he did was strictly because this country is moving toward socialism; the majority want the government to take care of them.

Numerous lawsuits have been generated pursuant to this recent presidential election fiasco in state and federal courts. You don't have to be a rocket scientist to ascertain for whom a court, say the Florida Supreme Court, is going to render its decision when the Florida Supreme Court justices were all appointed by Democratic governors.

---

[3] Orlando Business Journal 8/18/2000

That's right: all Florida Supreme Court Justices were appointed by Democrat Governors in Florida. And yes, this Court ruled in favor of Gore and the Democratic Party insofar as their petitions for recounting of the ballots, etc. Who was it that said "The law is politics in a costume"? Historically it has been proven that the justice (joke) system is liberal and politically Democrat in its rulings. The Lady of Justice standing on a platform with her eyes blind-folded in the best interests of justice, holding the scales of justice is a sick joke perpetrated on the American people. If you don't believe that then you are rather naive, my friend. I guess we Americans can be grateful that the U.S. Supreme Court finally came in and overturned the Florida Supreme Court's ludicrous decision in this presidential vote scenario. They ruled that the Florida Supreme Court was acting in the capacity of a legislative body instead of a judicial body and that they violated Constitutional issues. Even the U. S. Supreme Court voted along ideological, philosophical and political lines...5 to 4! While on this subject let me briefly bring up another example.

Remember the Linda Tripp situation where the government prosecutors were trying to get Ms. Tripp on some legal technicality for her part in helping expose President Clinton and his affair with Lewinsky? Initially a President Reagan appointed federal judge was appointed to hear the case. All of a sudden and without explanation the case was taken away from that judge and turned over to a three panel judgeship consisting of three federal judges all appointed by President Clinton.[4] Give me a break! Tell me this was coincidental. This poor lady never had a chance in fighting the system. This is one of hundreds of thousands of lawsuits and litigation that are decided by other than the means of law and justice. It's the "who you know" syndrome and you had better believe it. And you had better believe that it happens from the county court up to the Supreme Court.

The Legal Reformer in its Spring 2001 edition brings note to the Texas judiciary as follows. "A new report issued by Texans for Public Justice indicated that law firms that have donated money to Texas

---

[4] Orlando Sentinel 8/18/2000

Supreme Court judges election campaigns are more than four times as likely to have their cases reviewed by the Texas Supreme Court than firms that donated no money. While members of the court are dismissive of the findings, the report also noted that the likelihood of having a case heard by the court is directly proportional to the amount donated. The bulk of the money donated to judges' election campaigns in Texas comes from lawyers and law firms. From the findings in this report, that money appears to have been well spent."

In LEGAL WHORES I will try to give the reader exposure to the basics in forms and explanations relative to everyday litigation involving divorce, modifications, bankruptcy, appeals, small claims, garnishment, etc. Additionally and more importantly, I will expose the legal fraternity for what it is...an insatiable money eating machine, a cancer that devours all good and productive actions in its path. God, principal, integrity, credibility, and family are all a distant second to the acquisition of money by whatever means. The legal fraternity seem to take special delight in attacking those in our society that can not afford an attorney to represent them. Sick, isn't it? Read on...

ATTORNEY FEES

Lawyer fees are the heart and nerve center of the legal system in the United States. Legal fees are the alpha and omega, basis, apex, ultimate end, god, lubricant and definition of the laws in this country. It is said that any civilized country must be governed by laws in order that society may operate in an organized and sane manner. This is true only if those who control the defining and execution of said laws also control the monetary remuneration therein. If you don't believe me, pass a law where no attorney is permitted to earn over $20,000 a year in the practice of law. Or they can not charge over $20 an hour for their services. You would have instant, utter chaos in this country. I had one attorney tell me "the Bill of Rights is really a lawyer's right to bill!" He thought this was funny as hell.

I have a goodly number of attorney acquaintances, perhaps in excess of a hundred: some with whom I have a close personal relationship. Most are incompetent while two are decent family people. However, everyone of them would prostitute their daughters for a nickel...well, maybe some would want a dime. The fact of the matter is that money is the focal point and only criteria for existence in these attorney's vocation. I don't know what happens to certain seemingly idealistic youngsters once they finish law school, pass the Bar entrance exam and start practicing law in the mainstream of the legal fraternity. You hear or read about it every day in the media. Just recently, a State Supreme Court had to publicly reprimand two lawyers for passing out their cards and soliciting business at a memorial service for the relatives of the victims of an airplane accident that occurred only one week beforehand! Which brings to mind lawyer John O'Quinn, who earned

17

an estimated $40,000,000 from breast implant cases, who was one of the four Houston lawyers charged with illegally soliciting clients after the 1994 crash of USAir Flight 1016 near Charlotte, N.C.[5] Or how about the lawyers that pay police clerks to let them know immediately of automobile accidents so that they will be first to contact the people involved in an effort to represent them in the numerous lawsuits they are able to file. Just be involved in a "fender-bender" and watch how many phone calls and letters you immediately start receiving from lawyers wanting to represent you. Go down to the traffic court and watch these scum-bags plying their trade right in the court room. I've seem them going from seat to seat in the traffic violation courtroom telling defendants that they will represent them that day for a quick $50. I could write an entire book on the sleazy practices of lawyers trying to get clients but won't belabor the point here. Most folks already know of or have had first hand experience of this nature.

I guess I can't blame the legal profession totally for their insatiable appetite for money. We the people tend to get greedy also. Too many folks in this country want something for nothing. If a situation arises whereby the average dude might be able to sue somebody, anybody, and collect some funds for their effort, they usually do. This is usually true whether or not there is any justification for such litigation. Of course, the lawyers promote such scenarios by taking on cases on a contingency basis. Class action suits are a prime example of lawyers sucking money out of the system. A financial bonanza for attorneys have been the recent legal onslaught of the states to sue the tobacco companies. Usually the Governor, as is the case in our state, raises the issue of the great damage and costs inflicted upon the state's citizenry due to the effects of using tobacco. Then the state (Governor) hires a regiment of his buddy lawyers (those who raised the most campaign contributions for his election) to take on the bad guys, the tobacco companies. Never mind that nobody held a gun to the head of those having alleged tobacco diseases and made them use tobacco products for all of those years. And guess whose money pays the costs

---

[5] USA TODAY 4/18/97

and fees for all of those outside law firms that are suing the tobacco companies in the name of the state? It's your tax dollars, Mr. Citizen.

Yesterday I heard Russ Limbaugh over the radio talking about a convict in a Florida prison. Seems as though this convict sued the State of Florida because he could not stop smoking. He wanted the State to provide him with some sort of medical aid that would help him stop using tobacco products as they have been proven unhealthy. In the State's answer to this lawsuit, the State of Florida said that the convict was an adult who could make his own decisions and should shoulder the burden of quitting smoking on his own. This is the very opposite position of what the State of Florida said in their class action law suit against the tobacco companies. In their suit, the State said that tobacco was an addictive drug and that folks could not stop on their own accord. Therefore, the tobacco companies should give the State of Florida billions of dollars for legal fees and to cover costs of getting Floridians off tobacco and curing any tobacco caused ancillary health problems. Boy! In the legal vernacular this is "getting two bites at the apple", "having your cake and eating it too"! Like Russ Limbaugh said, it's based on nothing but money, money, money. Yes sir. Feed that legal fraternity...

Another financial smorgasbord for the legal fraternity I constantly witness is in the relatively small city or county. These governmental jurisdictions are usually too small to justify a full time legal department or lawyer as an employee. A law firm is chosen by the majority of the elected officials usually based on which lawyer raised the most campaign moneys for re-election for the majority of the incumbents. Legal competency is not a relevant factor here. If you don't believe this is what happens from a municipal level right on up to the Congress, then you are too naive to understand this book and need to start reading Donald Duck instead. Once in, the outside hired law firm has no incentive not to litigate their governmental entities' problems. The politicians that gave them the job are usually not lawyers themselves and therefore must believe the legal recommendations of their hired legal counsel. It's a financial dream come true for the attorneys. Some of the litigation instituted by these attorneys on behalf of their municipality/county is outright ludicrous. But it enhances their billing hours significantly and the poor, naive taxpayer who really pays the bill doesn't understand what the hell is going on anyway. The sad part of this whole scenario is that we are not talking about peanuts. Check out your local municipal, county, or state department budget to ascertain the legal costs (tax dollars) spent on legal representation. Look closely as some of it is most probably hidden under administration or some other surreptitious heading. Believe me, you are going to be shocked!

Here's a good example of what I mean. A small central Florida city has had the same outside attorney for over 16 years. The city has about the same population as the City of Sanford, just up the road. Sanford also has an outside city attorney. According to the Orlando Sentinel, the City of Sanford paid their city attorney an estimated $250,000 that year while this city paid its outside city attorney $1.4 million for various legal work for the city. Two years previously, this city gave their outside city attorney a three year contract without going out for bid. He charged $165 an hour (a lot of money back then) while the other cities in Seminole County were charged a maximum of $90 an hour for legal services by their respective outside city attorneys. Incidentally, the Orlando Sentinel stated this three year contract was awarded several months after the city manager and the city attorney bought some beach front property together as a partnership over on Florida's east coast. Yes, the city manager has been City Manager for about as long as this outside city attorney has been the city attorney. It is reported that this outside city attorney constantly wines and dines the city commission and is supported wholeheartedly by the majority of the five member city commission. What's that old saying..."3 votes out of 5 beats hell out of a good argument every time!"

Even if your local jurisdiction (city, county) has an in-house legal department, the situation often arises wherein a specialist is required. Usually this is on labor matters such as the fire department trying to go union or a fired employee suing for discrimination. These so-called specialists, e.g. labor attorneys, are very expensive. Nevertheless, payment for fund raising efforts are satisfied...

Have you ever hired an attorney that did not require a monetary retainer up front? If so, you'd better latch on to this dude as he is a rare breed. The lawyers always want to be paid for work yet to be done. In this manner they don't have to sue you for services rendered and not paid for. I like having a business where I get paid for my efforts and services before they are produced.

The so-called "billing hours" of a lawyer tend to be a joke in this day and age. Work that used to take me 8 hours to do, I can now accomplish in 15-30 minutes! Research is extremely easy and fascinatingly quick nowadays with the availability of computers, CD-ROM, modems, e-mail, and internet. Letters, forms, complaints, answers, motions, and a myriad of other documents, of local, state and federal origins, are available via computer disks, software or modems. The time required today to formulate any of these documents versus just 10 years ago is minuscule. Yet, today's "legal beagles" tend to keep billing their naive clients at the same old hourly billing time schedule and constantly get away with it. For example, I charge $275 total cost for a simplified dissolution of marriage (divorce) in my area, and it takes about 4-5 hours. It's a no-brainer fill in the blanks set of forms. The typical attorney in this area usually charges an average of $1,500 - $6,000 for the same action and takes 6 - 9 months. I guess it's great to pay your legal assistant $12 an hour to fill in the blanks on a form while you charge the client $200+ per hour for the same work: let's see, that's a $188+ an hour profit. Not bad...

Miscellaneous attorney fee mentions not involving class-action suits:

1. According to the 6/27/98 program JUSTICE FILES on the Discovery Television Channel, over $500,000,000 in legal fees alone have been paid by the Roman Catholic Church in addition to damages for sex abuse claims against priests.

2. The USA TODAY[6] quotes the Indianapolis Star newspaper in an editorial: "Lawyers are examining companies' liability if computers fail, the lights go out and shipments are missed. Other lawyers are preparing class-action lawsuits. Analysts estimate the Y2K litigation could run as high as $100,000,000,000...." When the year 2000 rolled

---

[6] 6/26/98

around, it would be a financial smorgasbord for the legal fraternity. Even the July 1998 issue of the Florida Trend magazine estimated that $10 would be spent on legal fees for every $1 spent to fix these computers. Florida Trend quoted Miami lawyer Mark Grossman as thinking that Year 2000 litigation would generate more lawsuits than the savings and loan crisis and asbestos cases combined. No wonder every kid on the block wants to be a lawyer; it's the money, stupid.

3. Orlando talk show host and all around political firebrand Doug Guetzloe filed a suit against his attorneys for over-billing. The headlines of the Orlando Business Journal[7] show WHEN $2,000 AN HOUR IS TOO MUCH. "They charged me for electricity," quipped Gurtzloe. He is appealing the legal fee award given by a lower court to the lawyers. Just another example of the good old boy syndrome of the ex-lawyer judges covering the practicing lawyers on legal fees.

4. Washington D. C. is a financial bonanza for lawyers. So many politicians are being investigated therefore requiring legal counsel in an effort to cover their butts that criminal defense attorneys are having a financial field day. I believe the majority of President Clinton's cabinet had been under criminal investigation at one time or other, requiring millions of dollars in criminal defense legal fees. President Clinton himself has spent millions of dollars in legal fees trying to cover his ass. This is just the tip of the iceberg! What about Monica Lewinsky, Linda Tripp, Paula Jones, etc., etc.? The New York Times[8] showed the following sums of money spent on some of these continuing investigations as of 4/6/97: (1) Whitewater...$30,100,000, (2) former Clinton Agriculture Secretary of Agriculture Mike Espy...$8,700,000, (3) former Clinton Commerce Secretary Ron Brown...$2,700,000, (4) former Clinton Housing Secretary Henry Cisneros...$2,300,000, (5) Iran-Contra...$62,400,000, (6) Watergate...$28,300,000. Colorado Democratic leader, Phil Perington, has said the (legal) furor "is slowing us down. People are very reluctant

---

[7] 7/25/97

[8] 4/6/97

to donate to this bottomless pit of attorneys' fees...that actually has nothing to do with the business of the country."[9] As of 11/97 the National Democratic Committee's legal costs relating to just the various fund-raising probes was $11,300,000.[10] One could probably write a book just on the organizations, politicians and bureaucrats that have been under investigation by the Justice Department, FBI or whomsoever during the Clinton years. I consider it poetic justice to have these politicians and bureaucrats, especially those that are attorneys, grovel and beg for moneys to cover their legal costs.

Here's another recent interesting Washington D. C. story that made the New York Times[11]. Former Congressman Robert K. Dorman of California had been defeated by a Loretta Sanchez. Dorman claimed the election was tainted by voter fraud and voting by non-citizens. The House Oversight Committee investigated. Thus far the Committee has spent $300,000, the Immigration and Naturalization Service has spent $150,000 and Ms. Sanchez has spent $400,000, all in legal fees. Ms. Sanchez retains her congressional seat and the New York Times very aptly suggested that in an effort to stop this madness of feeding the legal fraternity with bushels of money Mr. Dorman should try to win the next election to get his seat back.

5. Every once in a while, and I do mean rarely, a judge chastises a lawyer for overcharging a client. Usually the impetus for this action is the result of the news media making a big deal out of it. A local example involved Osceola County Judge Carol Draper and attorney J. Gordan Blau. Blau's clients were suing another party for $250. Blau charged them $20,362 in legal fees! Blau's clients balked and the judge said, "I honestly have never seen anything like this before...it is that outrageous." The judge sliced Blau's fee to $1,031 and $96.50 in costs for the $250 lawsuit.[12]

[9] USA TODAY 5/12/97

[10] USA TODAY 11/26/97

[11] 11/16/97

[12] Orlando Business Journal 6/9/95

6. British Virgin Airways owner, Richard Branson, sued renown U. S. lottery boss Guy Snowden in a libel suit. Branson won and was awarded $192,000 in damages by the jury. Branson estimated his legal fees at $1,600,000. [13]

7. As we all are aware, the government (local, state and federal) pays private attorneys with tax dollars to represent indigent folks in criminal cases. The amount given to these financially hungry legal beagles varies but is usually set by certain finite statutory limitations. The typical judge can and often does override the legislative maximums in these cases. For example, in MONROE COUNTY vs MANUEL E. GARCIA[14] Monroe County, Florida appealed the local judge's award of $21,347.50 to a private attorney for representing Mr. Garcia in a criminal case. Section 925.036(2)(c), Florida Statutes (1995) puts a statutory cap of $3,000 in legal fees in this particular situation. I can only surmise that this attorney was a good buddy or associate of the judge as $21,347.50 in anybody's arithmetic is a hell of a lot more than $3,000. Monroe County appealed this legal fee award to the 3rd District Court of Appeals of Florida, hanging their hat on the law... Section 925.036(2)(c), Florida Statutes (1995). The 3rd District Court of Appeals ruled, "We hold that a fee award in excess of the statutory limit is permissible when necessary to ensure effective representation." which I guess means we judges are gonna cover the brothers in their fee requests.

In another local case and much to the chagrin of Osceola County, the circuit judge awarded 2 attorneys representing an indigent criminal legal fees of $175,000.[15] Bend over Mr. & Mrs. Taxpayers, here it comes again.

---

[13] Orlando Sentinel 2/3/98

[14] 22 Fla. L. Weekly D1427

[15] Orlando Sentinel 11/28/96

8.   Clint Eastwood prevailed in his invasion of privacy suit against the National Inquirer, winning a $150,000 damage award. His lawyer fees were $653,000.[16]

9.   The 1996 Anderson Boyer Group/LOMAR Law Office Compensation Billing and Office Automation Survey states that the average hourly billing for lawyers of all concentrations for 1996 was $183 an hour. It would be interesting to see the results of this survey for this year after the awarding of legal fees in the recent numerous class-action suit settlements where **billions** of dollars have been awarded to the attorneys.

10.   The Florida Bar News[17] had an interesting letter to the editor from an attorney concerning hourly rates which I must share with you. He referred to an article in the Florida Bar News[18] concerning the efforts of the All Bar Conference to address the problems of middle-income people hiring attorneys. He quoted Michele Cummings, the chair of the Access to the Legal Systems Committee as saying the Bar "needs a campaign to publicize that there are lawyers out there for these people (lower-to-middle-income), these lawyers are willing to work for reasonable fees." This comment was in reference to a few lawyers who offered prices of less than $125 per hour or sliding-scale fees to people. According to the letter's author, attorney Roy L. Beach, "This tells me that the rest of Florida's attorneys are charging an unreasonable fee for services rendered and I think she (Michele Cummings) is right." Attorney Beach continues, "I spoke with an attorney who used to be in private practice and who now works for the government. He stated that he personally could not have been able to afford to hire an attorney who charges what he charged (when in private practice). If an attorney who charges $125 per hour for his time could not afford to hire another attorney for that same rate, how in God's name do we expect someone

---

[16] Orlando Sentinel 8/31/97

[17] 4/1/97

[18] 2/15/97

who earns $15 per hour to be able to afford an attorney?" Beach concluded by saying, "Is it any wonder that attorneys are perceived as money-hungry bandits who are no better than used car salesmen or politicians?" Now folks, this story is quoted directly from a letter to the editor by an attorney in the newspaper for Florida attorneys.

    11. The Orlando Sentinel newspaper[19] offered a front page story that is worth repeating. "Thousands of poor children needing day care in Florida are headed for a brick wall.... As of July 15, a group of state-backed insurance companies will stop writing homeowners policies for people caring for more than three children in their homes...." And why, you may ask? Seems as though your local, greedy attorneys have found another way to suck money out of the system. There has become such a plethora of lawsuits against the smaller, affordable child-care centers which poorer people can afford, that the insurance companies have banded together and decided not to insure them any more. There are just too many lawsuits where the legal fees and damage costs have gotten out of hand. "Insurance companies have a legitimate concern about being tagged with lawsuits involving child care.... Homeowners insurance companies have been successfully sued for injuries to children - even when the family child-care providers have separate liability insurance.... Several states have enacted legislation that preserves family child-care homes by protecting homeowners insurance companies from liability lawsuits." So what if poor folks don't have a place to put their small children during the day while they work for that enormous $5.75 an hour; what the hell does the legal fraternity care?

    Lawyers are always trying to create new ways to screw the public out of fees for themselves. The International Herald Tribune[20] tells this story on their front page. "More than a generation after civil rights and environmental lawyers took their battles to the courts, there are now lawyers who say they are following in those footsteps on behalf of clients with names like Freckie and Muffin and Rainbow. Fighting for

---

[19] 6/6/97

[20] 8/19/99

creatures like performing orangutans and dogs used in experimentation, the lawyers are creating a new field of animal law with far more ambitious goals than traditionally weak anti-cruelty laws. They are filing novel lawsuits producing new legal scholarship to try to chip away at a fundamental principle of American law: that animals are property and have no rights." This new avenue of law invented by the legal fraternity has and is adding millions of dollars annually to the lawyers pockets in the form of legal fees. Guess who ends up paying for all of this? Believe it or not, about a dozen law schools now teach animal law, including Harvard, Georgetown, the University of Vermont and the University of California at Los Angeles.[21]

12. The Florida Bar News[22], the mouth piece for Florida lawyers quoted one of the Florida Supreme Court Justices (Major Harding) as saying, "even members of our own legal community see unnecessary litigation and call family law a fee-generating machine." You know, it must really be bad when a member of the Supreme Court makes such a public statement. And the beat goes on...

---

[21] New York Times 8/22/99

[22] 8/1/2000

Legal Whores

Legal Whores

CLASS ACTION LITIGATION

If ever there was a financial smorgasbord for the legal fraternity, class action litigation is it. When a lawyer can find three or more individuals that claim they have been harmed or a law violated against them, then a class action lawsuit can be initiated against the alleged perpetrator on behalf of the plaintiffs plus the unlimited number of potential ancillary plaintiffs that might have been harmed accordingly by the defendant. Usually the greater the number of plaintiffs involved in a suit, the higher the settlement and likewise the higher the legal fees the attorney is able to extrapolate from the award. The trial lawyers in the United States have been able to get Congress to pass laws that generate a vast basis for initiating class action litigation in a myriad of unique ways. Sexual and racial discrimination lead the pack but then class action litigation such as product liability follow a close second. As the lawyers are well aware, class-action litigation is a "no brainer". Lawyer's computers churn out cookie-cutter lawsuits to be brought by his colleagues throughout the country. Many of these form lawsuits have been found to contain identical typographical errors even thought they were filed in different states.

The 6/23/97 edition of the USA TODAY Newspaper had an excellent article headed "Precedent could lead to suits in other industries". They were referring to the big legal fee billion dollar payoffs generated as a result of the tobacco litigation. It's a great article! "Who's next? Once the tobacco industry pays billions of dollars to settle...." the legal fraternity may begin to pressure other industries to defray medical costs and pay billions more in legal fees. "Makers of liquor may be a target. But no maker of an unhealthy product is safe,

29

not even makers of barbecue grills.... It's absolutely clear that charcoal broiling is carcinogenic." And there is no end to the possibilities: liquor (alcohol) is addictive to some users with painful results, fried food can cause heart trouble, milk contains fat which can clog the arteries for which a Washington man sued dairy farmers, and continuing ad infinitum. Just recently U. S. attorneys are opening offices in Europe and Asia in an effort to pursue class-action litigation in other countries.

Here are just a few examples of the thousands of recent class-action suits born out of the legal fraternity.

TEXACO
Alleged racial discrimination...1,342 folks averaged receiving $60,000 per person for a total of $115,000,000 plus **legal fees of $29,000,000.** However, before this class action suit was brought to its conclusion, TEXACO had shelled out a total of $176,000,000.[23]

AVIS RENTAL CAR
Alleged racial discrimination...Original plaintiffs were three black women. Award was $3,280,000 with approximately **$2,500,000** of the total going to the **lawyers for fees and costs.**[24]

SHELL OIL COMPANY ET AL
Product liability (leaky plastic pipes in mobile homes)...67,000 plaintiffs were awarded $750 each while the **lawyers got $109,000,000.**[25]

FIRST UNION BANK
Alleged age discrimination...239 former employees were awarded $59,000,000. Guess how much the lawyers sucked out of this one![26]

---

[23] USA TODAY 2/27/97 and 12/9/97.

[24] USA TODAY 12/23/97.

[25] USA TODAY 12/10/96.

[26] USA TODAY 10/23/97.

BARNETT RECOVERY CORPORATION

Alleged violation of the Federal Fair Debt Collection Practice Act (in other words, going after dead beat debtors who wouldn't pay their bills)...each class member awarded $15 and the estimated **legal payday for the attorney was $125,000.**[27]

PUBLIX SUPERMARKET STORES

Alleged racial and sex discrimination...34,000 women received $63,500,000 ($1,867 each), black employees got an extra $3,500,000 and the **lawyers picked up $18,000,000** for their efforts.[28]

CSX RAILROAD

Chemical leak from railroad car that allegedly started a fire (no fatalities incurred)...Fire was in a railroad yard and smoke drifted over to a neighboring residential subdivision. The Federal National Transportation Safety Board investigation found that CSX Railroad was not responsible for the chemical leak that caused the fire. However, the $3,500,000,000 judgment awarded to the plaintiffs in this class action lawsuit is 7 times the 1989 payout by Dupont for the chemical explosion at Bhopal, India that killed 3,000 people. Just imagine what the lawyers milked out of this one.[29]

ALL STATE INSURANCE COMPANY

Class action suit by its California agents to recover alleged unreimbursed business expenses. The settlement ended up being $25,000,000 with each agent receiving $10,000 and the **lawyers pocketing $7,500,000.**[30]

---

[27] Williams et al vs Barnett, Case No. 395CV01505PCD, US District Court of Connecticut.

[28] Orlando Sentinel 5/25/97.

[29] New York Times 9/14/97.

[30] USA TODAY 12/10/96.

BANCBOSTON BANK

Failure by BancBoston to pay interest in a timely manner on mortgage escrow accounts generated a $40,000,000 settlement wherein homeowners each got $9 and the **lawyers were paid $8,500,000** for their efforts. Incidentally, the $8,500,000 legal fees were taken out of an added interest fee of 5.32% subsequently placed on each homeowner's escrow account, costing some homeowners as much as $90.[31]

TOYOTA

Toyota was accused of inflating automobile prices by including an advertising cost in its dealer invoices in a unique class action suit dreamed up by an attorney. Some 3,000,000 Toyota customers were awarded a coupon good for $150 on their purchase of another Toyota auto. The **lawyers reaped in $4,250,000** for this class action idea.[32]

HOOTERS

Alleged sex discrimination...Hooters is a chain of bar and grill restaurants known for its macho setting, good food and drinks and pretty, well endowed waitresses. Some lawyer got several males to apply for jobs as waiters who were turned down and then filed a class action suit. Result was $2,000,000 to the plaintiffs not to exceed $19,100 to any one plaintiff and a **$1,750,000 legal fee** payment to the lawyer.[33]

PRUDENTIAL INSURANCE COMPANY OF AMERICA

Alleged "churning" of policies by its agents by persuading customers to use their built-up cash value of older life insurance policies to finance more expensive ones. Settlement was $2,000,000,000 to be split up

---

[31] USA TODAY 12/10/96.

[32] San Francisco Examiner 9/27/97.

[33] USA TODAY 11/1/97.

among thousands of policy holders while the **lawyers received $90,000,000 in legal fees.**[34]

UNITED PARCEL SERVICE
Alleged sex discrimination...a former United Parcel Service manager was awarded $80,700,000 by a jury. And what do you think her attorney got?![35]

DOW CORNING
Alleged product liability...breast implants...Settlement was $2,800,000,000. **Lawyer fees will range from a low of $280,000,000 to a maximum of $840,000,000.** Can you guess what the final legal bill will end up being?[36] Dow Corning was forced into bankruptcy because of this legal abortion. Incidentally, subsequent medical tests have proven that the silicon implants were not the cause of the alleged injury in this case.

PHARMACISTS
Pharmacists sued drug manufacturers in an antitrust suit...Settlement of $408,000,000 which provided **$122,000,000 in legal fees.**[37]

U.S. DEPT. OF AGRICULTURE
Pending racial discrimination class action suit by 350 black farmers asking for $2,500,000,000. Who do you really think is going to win this one and what will the lawyers suck out of this one? [38]

---

[34] Orlando Sentinel 3/21/97.

[35] USA TODAY 5/27/98.

[36] USA TODAY 8/29/97.

[37] USA TODAY 12/10/96.

[38] USA TODAY 3/6/98.

STATE FARM INSURANCE COMPANY
Sex discrimination class action suit...Settlement of $250,000,000 with legal fees of $65,000,000.[39]

SHONEY'S RESTAURANTS
Racial discrimination class action suit...Settlement of $132,500,000 with legal fees of $20,000,000. [40]

LUCKY'S GROCERY STORES
Sex discrimination class action suit...Settlement of $107,000,000 with legal fees of $10,000,000. [41]

U.S. ARMY CORPS OF ENGINEERS
Sex discrimination suit by 50 black employees...Settlement of $389,000 plus legal fees.[42]

STATE OF FLORIDA
Courts agree with class action litigation lawyers that 37,000 minors in the custody of the State of Florida have a right to file a class action suit against the State for not receiving the "help" they need: whatever that means. Anyway, this litigation probably will end up costing the taxpayers hundred of millions of dollars in settlement and legal fees.[43]

---

[39] Orlando Sentinel 1/25/97.

[40] Orlando Sentinel 1/25/97.

[41] Orlando Sentinel 1/25/97.

[42] Orlando Sentinel ½/97.

[43] Orlando Sentinel 4/4/97.

GANGSTER

Convicted and incarcerated well known gangster is writing a book which looks like it might generate significant sums of money for the gangster. In the book, gangster tells how he murdered a number of folks. Lawyer got together the families of a dozen of the murdered victims and filed a class action suit against the gangster and his estate. Some lawyers have an uncanny ability to smell out that possible dollar. Incidentally, all of the murdered victims above were alleged members of crime families themselves.[44]

U.S. FEDERAL RESERVE BANK OF CHICAGO

Pending racial discrimination class action suit by 20 black past and present employees and their lawyer. Open your wallets, Mr. Taxpayer.[45]

NATIONAL CAR RENTAL

Pending racial discrimination class action suit by 9 black individuals and their lawyer. Watch the cost of renting a car go up.[46]

MORTGAGE FIASCO

A Dexter J. Kanidewiaz of Maine was a class action winner in a suit involving mortgage escrow accounts. His winnings: $2.19; his legal bill: $91.33.[47]

The lawyers have now graduated to a higher level of class action litigation wherein they don't have to mess with the lowly hundreds of millions of dollars in legal fees any more. The lawyers have started going after large and well financed corporations pursuant to their products. The first biggie was the tobacco companies. Let's take Florida as an example as to how it is done.

---

[44] DATELINE 4/8/98.

[45] USA TODAY 2/26/98.

[46] USA TODAY 7/9/97.

[47] New York Times 2/23/97.

First, as a lawyer, you help elect the Governor and make sure he is owing to you and realizes that you were instrumental in his election. Next find some large and well financed corporation that has a product that can be construed as being detrimental to the public at large, such as the tobacco companies and their tobacco products. Convince the Governor that a class action suit against this corporation will make the Governor look great politically and a savior of the people. Simultaneously, have the Governor, as the Chief Executive of the State, execute a legal fee contract with you wherein you get a set percentage of the total settlement for your efforts. This usually runs 25 - 40%. File your class action suit against the nasty corporations on behalf of the State while the Governor via the news media tells all of his voters how he is saving them from terrible tobacco and is suing for money to improve their health status. Now everybody loves the Governor who is looking out for their health. Give me a break! You've got to be pretty damn naive to believe this crap. The first, foremost and most important concern are the legal fees being generated in this action. It's political payoff time, sports fans! Governor Lawton Chiles of Florida, an attorney, pulled this scenario off with great showmanship during his tenure.

TOBACCO CORPORATIONS

Numerous states have filed class action suits on behalf of their citizens decrying the health effects of tobacco products. Lawyers who have sued the tobacco industry on behalf of states stand to collect **legal fees of between $7,900,000,000 and $18,000,000,000**, legal scholars told a congressional panel December 10, 1997.... Folks, that's **BILLIONS**, not **MILLIONS**! In Florida, some of the lawyers hired by the state were seeking fees that would work out to more than **$7,700 an hour**....and they got it. Lester Brickman, a professor at Brandeis University's Cardozo School of Law, testified that the fee agreements with the states, if enforced as written, would generate **legal fees of $18,600,000,000**. That would be more than the nation's top 100 law firms earned last year, he said.[48] In the 12/10/97 edition of the USA

---

[48] USA TODAY 12/11/97.

TODAY newspaper, respected media writer, Walter Schapiro stated, "Already the trial lawyers are greedily emulating sports stars and corporate CEOs by claiming as much as 25% of Florida's independent settlement with the tobacco companies." According to the 10/5/97 New York Times the Florida tobacco attorneys have already started filing legal fee liens against the tobacco moneys the State is supposed to get to insure they get their fees. Judge H. J. Cohen calculated attorney fees in the Florida tobacco agreement at $7,716 an hour, if the lawyers worked on the case every hour of every day since the case began. [49] The legal fees in the Florida tobacco settlement are estimated at $2,800,000,000. Just to let you know how the legal fraternity puts things into perspective, the Judge said he could see hundreds of millions of dollars for these legal fees but not billions. It's really a moot point because in June of 1998 an appellate court in Florida ruled that the Judge in the circuit court had no right limiting the tobacco legal fees as the lawyers had a valid contract with the State of Florida.[50] And to re-emphasize how greedy these typical lawyers are, the FLORIDA TREND MAGAZINE (2/98) said that the 11 trial lawyers in the Florida tobacco case are in a "slugfest" among themselves over the $2,800,000,000 legal fees. Florida State Senator Tom Lee, R-Brandon, a member of the Senate Select Committee on Tort Reform said, "If there ever was a poster child for the need for litigation reform, this is it." Even a poll by the Orlando Sentinel[51] showed that 93% of those calling in said the lawyers should not get even a billion dollars from the tobacco settlement. (Late note: radio station WDBO announced that the private lawyers in the Florida tobacco case were just awarded $3,400,000,000 in legal fees).[52]

Not to be outdone by the Florida lawyers, a federal judge okayed the Texas lawyers' $15,300,000,000 tobacco settlement for

---

[49] USA TODAY 12/9/97.

[50] Kerrigan Et Al v State of Florida, 23 Fla. L. Weekly D1243.

[51] 9/3/97

[52] 12/12/98

Texas with a nice **legal fee** of $2,300,000,000 (folks, these are billions...not millions) for themselves.

The United States Senate (mostly lawyers) took up the issue of putting a cap on the tobacco class-action legal fees. There was talk of a cap of $6,500,000,000. [53] But no, the issue was dropped in an effort to let the legal fraternity milk as much money as possible out of the tobacco fiasco.

FLORIDA FIRES

I would like to pass another "can you top this" on to you that I heard over the radio. Right now the worst fires in Florida's history are just subsiding. Approximately 500,000 acres have burned, mainly in the Flager-Volusia-Brevard-Marion County areas. Thirty-seven homes burned in a subdivision in Flagler County called Seminole Woods. They burned in spite of the valiant efforts of local firefighters and firefighters from 41 states. Nevertheless, some smart lawyer has convinced these 37 homeowners to let him represent them and file a class action suit against all of the governmental entities and organizations who were involved in fighting the fires. The Plaintiffs' cause of action is that the Defendants could have prevented these fires had they acted in a responsible manner. Probable outcome is that the Defendants will settle out of court paying with taxpayers' dollars and, once again, the lawyers will feast upon the public financial trough.

WENDY'S

Today I heard that a group of minorities are filing a class-action suit against WENDY'S for discrimination. I never looked at ole Dave Thomas the CEO who is the gentle fellow in the WENDY television commercials as a white sheet totin' Klan supporter. Anyway, some attorney convinced some blacks that WENDY'S was discriminating against them and there might be some money in it for them, They have filed a $150,000,000 class action lawsuit against WENDY'S in the federal courts. These lawyers ought to make a bundle on this one!

---

[53] USA TODAY 3/30/98.

38

FIREFIGHTERS

Closer to home in Orange County, Florida a lawyer convinced 32 white county firefighters that they were discriminated against when they were passed over for promotion in favor of less qualified black firefighters. A class action lawsuit was filed against the county for $5,000,000 for emotional harm, $1,000,000 for lost wages and $2,000,000 for attorney fees.[54] Orange County settled out of court for $1,500,000 of taxpayer's money. $500,000 went to the 32 firefighters ($15,625 each) and $1,000,000 went to the attorney for legal fees. Is this a great country or what!

GUNS...GUNS...GUNS

Heard over the radio that the City of New Orleans had their private attorneys file a class-action lawsuit against the gun manufacturers. They are patterning their class-action suit after the tobacco class-action suits. They claim it is the gun manufacturers' fault that folks get injured with guns. This action ought to make a few more attorneys billionaires before it's over. Kind of reminds me of the one where the Florida Supreme Court put Kmart Corp. back on the hook in a $12,000,000 liability case brought by a woman shot and paralyzed by a drunken ex-boyfriend shortly after he bought a rifle at a Tampa Kmart. It's a decision one lawyer claims raises the specter of retailers giving their customers sobriety tests. Anyway, the woman was awarded $12,000,000 at the circuit court level but the award was overturned at the 4th District Court of Appeals level. On appeal the Florida Supreme Court saw it differently wherein they held this woman's case "falls squarely within traditional and well-established principles of common law negligence in Florida." Subsequently, Jacksonville attorney Jack Shaw, who represented the Florida Retail Federation, the International Mass Retail Association and the National Sporting Goods Association in this case, said the Supreme Court's opinion has given the retailers of everything

[54] Orlando Sentinel 10/12/98.

from chain saws to pool-cleaning acid something to worry about.[55]   I would guess that the next class-action suit will be against the automobile manufacturers in that they are responsible for the zillions of dollars expended annually pursuant to accidents, injuries and deaths.

CORPORATE STOCKS
Once again lawyers have found a source from which to line their pockets. This one is the corporate business industry. As most of us realize, purchasing stocks in a corporation is a usually a financial gamble at best. For example, the shares of Citrix recently dropped by more than 45% when the company cut its second quarter earnings estimates to between 9 and 11 cents per share. A year earlier it earned 16 cents for the quarter. The consensus estimate had been 21 cents per share. Currently trading at about $24, the stock has a 52 week high of 122. Last week (6/2000) the company became the target of a shareholders suit. The lawyers are requesting class-action status and will probably get it. According to Lauren Rudd of the USA TODAY, "My experience has been that such suits result in tremendous fees for the lawyers, which is why they are filed." [56]

MISCELLANEOUS [57]
The tobacco settlement promises to be the richest payoff to trial lawyers on record, Here are some of the records it may break:
   * **For a single case:** $1 billion to plaintiffs' lawyers for the Exxon Valdez oil spill in Alaska.
   * **For a single lawyer:** $400 million to Joseph Jamail for winning the Pennzoil Co. suit against Texaco in the mid-1980s.
   * **For health problems caused by a particular product:** $1 billion or more for asbestos claims in 200,000 cases. Many are still being litigated.

---

[55] Florida Trend 10/97.

[56] USA TODAY 6/18/2000.

[57] USA TODAY 12/9/97.

But in one suit involving only 14,000 asbestos victims, lawyers were awarded $70,000,000 in fees.

Some **attorney awards** in other controversial cases:

* $90,000,000 plus $20,000,000 from settlement of defective Dalkon Shield birth control device case against A. H. Robins.

* $49,000,000 in settlement of flight attendants' suit against tobacco companies for exposure to secondhand smoke.

* $43,000,000 from settlement of leaky plastic pipe case against Shell Oil, Hoechst Celanese and DuPont.

* $29,000,000 from settlement of racial discrimination claims against Texaco.

* $10,000,000 from settlement of Bjork-Shiley heart valve case.

The above stories are just a minuscule number of actual class-action suits that have been filed in the United States. It would take a novel by itself to identify the number of on-going class-action litigation in this country.

Standby for stories soon in the media from Europe and Asia involving class-action litigation initiated by U. S. Legal beagles. It has already started in Japan and England!

Legal Whores

DIVORCE

The majority of civil cases in the Florida court system are in some way affiliated with Chapter 61, Florida Statutes, the family law statute. This law encompasses divorce (known as dissolution of marriage in Florida), child custody, child support, alimony, adoption...anything to do with the family short of criminal actions. Chapter 61, Florida Statutes is a financial bonanza for the legal fraternity in not only the State of Florida but the entire nation. Firstly, any action under the Family Law Statute tends to generate emotional feelings. The parties are prone to react with their emotions rather than with their good common sense. Attorneys are well aware of this scenario and take advantage of it. Emotions and non-familiarity with the legal system by the parties are the mainstays of lawyers' rise to financial prominence in family law. A good example is the one which I previously touched on in the dedication. An elderly German couple came to my office and asked what it would cost for a non-contested divorce with no minor children involved and how long would it take. They had already split their assets pretty much evenly. Their total assets were in excess of a million dollars. After asking them some preliminary basic questions, I informed them at the time that I would charge $150 for all of the paper work, that the filing fee would be $130 and it would take about 4 to 6 weeks to get their final judgment. (This was before Judge SB and Judge NB were put in the Family Division where this same scenario then started taking 3 to 9 months.) The man said, "But you don't understand. We just left Mr. Attorney's office and he quoted us $5,000 and said it would take 6 months for the final judgment". On further questioning I found out that this lawyer quoted them the $5,000 fee after he found out what their assets were. I told this 62 year old gentleman and his 60 year old wife that it was them that didn't understand. Welcome to the real world of the legal fraternity. Once the attorney finds out what your assets are, he will milk the case for all it is worth. Ask O. J. Simpson.

It is really funny to hear people say that their attorney is not like this; that their attorney treats them right and is competent and never over charges them. This same philosophy sort of reminds me of a nationwide poll taken a number of years ago by one of the major media networks. Paraphrasing the question asked, the media asked what would you advise being done to turn this country around in lowering the deficit and enhancing a better value system? The vast majority answered by saying, we should replace all of those congressman and senators in Washington, D. C. .....except mine! How do you reason with folks like that?#&*

Incompetency is another virtue that runs rampant in the legal fraternity. Just because a person has passed the State Bar exam or is a judge does not qualify him as a mental giant or a purveyor of legal knowledge in the field of family law or whatever legal discipline is involved. I remember back in the early 1980s when the American Bar Association had its annual convention in San Francisco and one of the speakers was the Chief Justice of the U. S. Supreme Court. He proclaimed that in excess of 80% to 90% of all lawyers in this country were incompetent. Some of the pleadings generated by attorneys which cross my desk every day are rather humorous...and pitiful. Humorous from the point of view of the number of mistakes made in the pleading, both objective and subjective: pitiful from the point of view that some poor naive bastard is the attorney's client and is paying him a handsome fee.

Please don't forget that lawyers are like physicians, they don't know every aspect of the law. Don't hire a criminal lawyer for a residential eviction. Don't hire a brain surgeon to give you a flu shot.

Many jurisdictions have law libraries within the public library. If they won't let you into the law library because you are not an attorney, find out if there are any public funds used in supplying the law library with books, personnel, or anything for that matter. If public funds are being utilized in the operation of the public library, there is your entree.

If they still won't let you in, go to your local newspaper editor, county commissioner or supervisor or local tax watch group and let your feelings be known in as strong a fashion as possible. You'll get into the law library. The reason you want to get into the law library is because you have now found the motherlode of the legal fraternity. Some law libraries are significantly better stocked than others but it sure beats hell out of none at all. Here you should find your State Rules of Civil Procedure. You are probably not qualified to do any significant legal research but you can understand and learn a great deal from such references as, for example, The Florida Legal Secretary. There are four volumes in this set meticulously covering such topics as dissolution of marriage (divorce), corporate law, landlord/tenant law and criminal law among others. The volumes are great in that they tell you exactly what to do and how to do it with examples. Many legal secretaries throughout the United States keep this set in their office for quick reference of their respective states' procedures. Remember, you are not an attorney and these references do not cover all situations. Be cautious. But if you cannot afford an attorney and the other party is about to tear your ass apart in court, I guess you really have no other alternate except to roll over and play dead. Most librarians will be most helpful in your legal endeavors but, believe me, they have been warned not to be too helpful to Pro Se Litigants. Once again, this is where a competent independent paralegal can be worth his weight in gold.

Okay, let's get down to business. If you and your spouse want a divorce, you agree on all matters and there are no minors nor assets involved, it's a slam dunk. In fact, some of your courthouses (Clerk's offices) will supply you and your spouse with the appropriate papers to file for a nominal charge. You will have to pay a filing fee unless you are indigent (no money or assets) in which case they normally will wave the filing fee. No further explanation is required in this situation.

Even if you all do have assets and you amicably divide them via a proper property settlement agreement, you can incorporate this agreement in the aforementioned paperwork supplied by the Clerk's office in most instances. Save your money and keep lawyers out of it. If distribution of the marital assets involves a pension or pre-marital assets or alimony or child support or something in which you don't feel comfortable doing by yourself, hire an attorney (or competent independent paralegal) for an hour to get your questions answered. Make sure all of your questions are written down before your appointment. If the attorney starts giving you some song and dance routine, get up and walk out. Find another lawyer. Please don't be intimidated by attorneys. If you are paying them, they are the *employee* and you are the *employer*. And there are a hell of a lot of them available out there. Just look in the yellow pages.

In Florida, if minor children are involved in a dissolution of marriage action, the parties might be limited by the papers supplied by the Clerk's office in the court house. If both parties are amenable and reside within the same state, your best bet is to find a competent independent paralegal to do the necessary paper work or you can investigate the law library previously mentioned in an effort to go it on your own. Remember, the paralegal cannot go to court and represent you. He can only prepare the documents for you to file. If you can read and walk and chew gum at the same time, you can do this. In Florida, the typical appropriate documents required for a non-contested dissolution of marriage in this situation include the Summons, Certificate of Service, Process Service Memorandum, Petition for Dissolution of Marriage, Financial Affidavits, Notice of Hearing (pre-trial conference and trial), Non-Military Affidavit, Corroborating Witness Affidavit and incorporated in the Final Judgment should be the property settlement agreement and any other nuances required by the local administrative procedures and guidelines. Add minor children to the divorce and you must include such additional documents as Uniform Child Custody Jurisdiction Act, Child Support Guidelines Worksheet, Notice to Payor, and Income Deduction Order in addition to the visitation rights of the non-custodial parent being incorporated into the Final Judgment. With no minor children but with alimony you can delete the Uniform Child Custody Jurisdiction Act and Child Support Guidelines Worksheet and any reference to visitation in the Final Judgment from the previous sentence. The Certificate of Service and Process Service Memorandum which are needed for service on the Respondent by the local Sheriff can usually be replaced with a Waiver of Service and Acknowledgment document notarized and executed by the Respondent. The Petitioner files with the Clerk's office at the court house all of the above completed documents. When you tell the Clerk that you are handling your own service, they will hand you back a Summons stamped by the Clerk and a Petition. You give these documents (Summons and Petition) to your spouse. After receiving copies of the stamped Summons and Petition from you, the Petitioner, your spouse should give you the executed and notarized Waiver of Service and Acknowledgment The executed Waiver of Service and Acknowledgment must then be filed with the Clerk. All of this action should take place in no longer a period of time than 120 days. Of course, it can also be done in one day. Typically a phone call to the judge's assistant or Pro Se Coordinator several days after your last filing of documents (Waiver of Service and Acknowledgment) should get you a hearing time and date. The assistant will ask of you the style of the case which will be the parties' names in a divorce and also she will ask for the case number. Certain judicial assistants do not like to talk to Pro Se Litigants and will give you a hard time. They might tell you to hire an attorney. If they refuse to give you a hearing, you are being denied "due process" as guaranteed by the U. S. Constitution. In an effort to cover your rear when dealing with these unhelpful court personnel, I would advise you to first write a letter (certified mail return receipt requested) directly to the judge of your case and tell him you are ready for trial, his judicial assistant is denying you due process by not giving you a hearing and demand a hearing date. Wait a week or two and call his judicial assistant again for a hearing date. If you still get the same treatment from the judge's secretary (judicial assistant), you should report them to the Chief Judge of the Circuit immediately. If the Chief Judge affords you no relief, you may have to file a formal complaint with the State Supreme Court or the judicial qualification committee or whoever is the authoritative body to handle such complaints in your state. Raise hell! Don't roll over and play dead. Even if your documents are not exactly proper according the Rules of Civil Procedure and the local administrative guidelines, the U. S. Supreme Court has directed that a Pro Se Litigant is not to be held to the same technical level as an attorney. They can't incarcerate you for demanding your rights. Afraid the judge will deny you the divorce? Baloney! He's more concerned about teeing off at 1:30 P.M. with his attorney buddy then your case. You are an inconsequential Joe Sixpack to him.

I recall a simple, non-contested dissolution of marriage action back in 1992. In Case No. 92-4554-DR-02-B a young lady, Petitioner, came to me to prepare the proper documents to file for divorce. The documents we use are those which have been approved by the Florida Supreme Court for just this purpose. All the proper documents were filed with the court, the spouse was served, there was no answer and a default was entered and a hearing date received. Judge JS was the presiding judge. The final judgment hearing was a slam dunk and should have taken no more than 30 seconds. As is any Pro Se Litigant representing themselves, this young lady was scared to death and very nervous. At the hearing, Judge JS called her before the bench and started yelling and cursing at her. He told her the documents were not correct and that she should go hire an attorney and to get the hell out of his court. I have an affidavit verifying this action. The young lady came back to my office crying. We immediately had our client file a Motion For Recusal (disqualification) of the judge with the appropriate accompanying documentation (affidavit and order). The judge recused himself. You see, the judge was absolutely wrong and he knew it. The Florida Supreme Court approved forms did have a mistake in that in the relief section it did not actually seek relief or specifically ask for a dissolution of marriage. But my client produced case law stating that even though a Florida Supreme Court approved form is not perfect and may lack certain specifics, the trial court shall not withhold affirmation due to this factor. It is the intent in these forms, not the format that rules. Subsequently, months later this young lady was granted her divorce by a different judge who accepted the originally filed documents.

The sad part of the above scenario is threefold. Firstly, the judge wanted this person to needlessly contribute to the legal fraternity by paying some scum bag attorney a couple of thousand dollars to finalize the dissolution of marriage. Ludicrous! Our office has used these same identical Florida Supreme Court approved forms hundreds of previous times throughout Florida with no problems whatsoever as to their validity and acceptability.

Secondly, the judge treated this young lady like dirt. I personally know this judge. He loves to throw his power around, especially when a party appears before him without an attorney. He forgets that the Joe Sixpack is paying his salary through taxes. Treating Pro Se Litigants with due respect is not in his vocabulary. I guess this is just another good example of voters really not knowing who they are putting in a judicial office. Fear not though, my friend, re-election time is soon and, finally, this Joe Sixpack is politically organized. Do we have some surprises for several local judges! Like Texas Bix Bender says, "There never was a horse that couldn't be rode; there never was a man that couldn't be throwed".

Thirdly, this action by the above judge ended up costing this young lady thousands of dollars anyway which she really could not afford. She had gone to contract to purchase a small condominium right after she filed for divorce. Closing was scheduled four months after she had filed for her simple, non-contested divorce. Typically, this was more than ample time to be awarded a final judgment in a simple non-contested dissolution of marriage in this jurisdiction. However, after being jerked around by the judge, she was not able to honor the original closing date on the condominium before her final judgment was given. This was important as she was taking title to the condominium in her maiden name which the court would award in her final judgment. She could not get an extension on her closing. She did not want to close and have the condominium conveyed into her married name prior to the final judgment as then the condominium could become part of the marital assets to which her spouse would legally have an equitable right to. Her only option in closing was to have title conveyed to her mother. Then after her final judgment her mother conveyed title back to her. The additional costs what with documentary stamps, hassles with the mortgage company and closing agency, etc. were nearly overwhelming for this little lady. All of this because some judge with an inferiority complex wanted to exercise his might in addition to enhancing the money coffers of his brethren in the legal fraternity. Believe me, if this lady had an attorney representing her initially, this occurrence never would have happened. I have seen too many similar happenings where the judge overlooked discrepancies in documents prepared by attorneys while denying Pro Se Litigants for the same or similar discrepancies.

In the above example I used the term default. I will define it later on.

Here is another example of a judge needlessly giving a Pro Se Litigant a hard time (Case No. 95-2915). A middle aged man came to our office for help in filing a simple, non-contested dissolution of marriage. His wife was in the military and stationed out of the country. There were no minor children involved and limited property. We prepared all of the required documents and referred to the Sailors and Soldiers Act as is required in cases where one of the spouses is on active duty in the military. The property settlement agreement was mailed to the wife for her signature and subsequent filing with the other documents. It is rather time consuming when mailing documents internationally. Once we had all the required documents signed and notarized, the husband filed them at the courthouse. Since he was handling his own service, he received the stamped Summons and Petition back from the Clerk and mailed them to his wife with the Answer and Waiver and Acknowledgment document. She executed this document, had it notarized and mailed it back to her husband, the Petitioner. The husband filed it at the court house and requested a hearing for the final judgment. In this case Judge SB determined on his own that he wasn't satisfied with the notarization of the parties' signatures on the property settlement agreement. This was perplexing to us. Having no alternative, we mailed the property settlement agreement internationally again to the wife for another notarized signature. The husband filed this completed agreement once again with the Clerk. Next, the judge would not accept the proposed final judgment because it referenced the property settlement agreement as an attachment; the judge wanted it incorporated in the body of the final judgment. We complied with the judge's demand. The judge also required that the husband now mail the proposed final judgment to the wife for her approval. Again, this was another new procedure we had never heard of. What else could this Pro Se Litigant do but comply? Finally, the judge granted the Husband/Petitioner a final judgment. This judge subjected this Petitioner to a lot of unnecessary, time consuming harassment. There was no legal basis for the requirements this judge set before the Pro Se Litigant in order for him to get his dissolution of marriage. Historically, Judge SB and his cronies on the bench have been known to openly discriminate against Pro Se Litigants. What recourse do these poor litigants have? They can't afford a lawyer and they certainly don't understand the system and procedures.

I have literally thousands of examples from which to draw for this book. But I am arbitrarily picking just certain causes in order to give you a basic idea as to what is going on and what you might possibly anticipate in your specific action. These are Florida based cases but some modification of them relative to your specific State's rules and laws might keep you from walking into the legal fraternity's lair totally and naively unarmed.

Case No. DR-94-8274 is where a husband, the Petitioner, hired a lawyer to file for a contested dissolution of marriage with no minor children involved. The marital assets were contested. After being served with the Summons and Petition by a Deputy Sheriff, the Respondent, a middle aged woman, came to us for help. She was unemployed, had no resources whatsoever, and the least expensive attorney she could find to help her in this action wanted $700 up front retainer for openers. She did not have anywhere near this amount. We quoted her $145 to handle the entire action and she could pay as she got the money.

We knew that she needed to answer the Petition for Dissolution of Marriage within twenty days of her being served with it or the other party would file a default. A default in essence means if you fail to timely (within twenty days of being served) answer the petition, the other party is in an excellent posture to be awarded by the trial court that which that party requested in the Petition. Usually the Clerk of the Court can issue a default but in some jurisdictions the judge wants to control this action. We didn't know from where the husband got his attorney. We did know that the attorney apparently didn't know what he was doing in this action. The petition was a joke. In addition to the form of the subject matter of this two page petition being poor, there was no case number on the document. As usual the petition contained several statements that were outright lies. It is common knowledge in the legal fraternity that you can lie like hell in a petition and it is up to the other party to prove you lied...errrr, I mean were misunderstood. In this case the petition stated that there were "no property or debt issues to be resolved in this action" and "the parties have executed a Marital (property) Settlement Agreement dated March 29, 1994, which disposes of all issues in this marriage". Both statements were false! Mr. I Q Attorney did not ask for fees and costs in his client's initial pleading either. What the hell does he care? He's going to get paid, regardless. The husband requested a dissolution of marriage and all the assets, etc.

Now you've got to realize that this woman has been an unemployed housewife at the request of her husband. She has nothing: he controls all the family assets, cash and all assets. The marital home is solely in his name as are certain rental properties and other real and personal properties. His income from various sources exceeds $100,000 a year. Also, he is on the drug Prozaic and other psychological prescription drugs.

Much to the Petitioner and his attorney's surprise, the wife, in a timely manner files an answer and counter-petition via our office. In her counter-petition the wife requests among other things, (1) the marital residence with the husband paying the mortgage and related costs for a period of four years, (2) rehabilitative alimony for a period of four years so that the wife could prepare herself for self support (she has no higher education nor license or trade on which to become employed), (3) equitable distribution of all marital assets. She had never signed a marital settlement agreement as stated in the husband's petition.

As expected, next comes the flurry of motions and requests from the husband's attorney. Remember, this woman literally has no assets. But this scum bag lawyer has got to generate spent time in order to justify the time he is charging the husband. Firstly, there is the Request for Production of Documents directed to the wife. Requested are a myriad of financial documents and data including but not limited to "federal income tax returns for the past three years", "records reflecting gross income and net income received either directly or indirectly for the current year and the past three years", "any financial statements prepared within the last five years in your possession or control". A ridiculous request, as the attorney knows fully well that this lady is broke and has no assets. The wife countered with an Objection to Request to Produce and Motion for Protection. The attorney got the judge to deny her request.

Next the husband told the wife to move out of the marital residence. She had nowhere to go and couldn't afford an apartment. Nearly simultaneously, the attorney filed a Motion for Exclusive Occupancy of the marital residence and the wife filed a Motion for Eviction of the husband from the marital residence. In addition, the wife filed a Motion for Temporary Alimony. Since her husband cut her off from any source of funds, she could not pay any of her bills or buy food. At the hearing on these motions the attorney got the judge to deny all of her motions. The judge gave her several days to vacate the marital residence. We knew this Orange County circuit judge was very anti-Pro Se :Litigant, so initially the wife had filed a Motion for Change of Venue in an effort to get to a more sympathetic forum. The parties resided in Seminole County and the petition was filed in Orange County. Proper and legal venue was where the parties last resided as husband and wife, that being Seminole County. Guess what! The judge illegally denied this motion. There is little doubt that an appeal to the Fifth District Court of Appeals would overturn the judge's venue ruling but who has thousands of dollars for legal fees and six to twelve months to kill. The wife was extremely distraught. She told me that she was going to throw in the towel and let nature take its course. I can not tell you how this one ended as we never heard from either of the parties again. Incidentally, we were never paid for our efforts and put the invoice with the rest of our ever growing pro bono work.

I would like to discuss process of service briefly. When an entity (person, corporation, whatever) is involved in or a party to a legal action in this country, it is their right of due process to be informed of such action. Their being informed is called service of process. As with the other terms in this primer, books have been written on service of process. For our purposes I will briefly define it. Usually the local Sheriff or his agent will serve the Defendant (Respondent or receiving party) with the petition and summons. This action puts one on notice that they have a time certain in which to answer the given allegations. If you fail to answer, the summons should fully explain the consequences. Service can be made anywhere in the world but I won't detail that action here. Service within the United States is fairly easy. Just phone the Sheriff's Department in the locale where you want the petition to be served and find out the cost and required procedure. When doing your own service, mail the stamped summons, petition and any other applicable documents (check and cover letter) to that particular Sheriff certified mail, return receipt requested. After serving the other party the summons and petition, the Sheriff will mail you back an affidavit affirming service. You are to file this affidavit in the courthouse. Make sure you keep a copy for yourself in case the Clerk's office loses the affidavit of service. As you will recall, I previously told you in a non-contested dissolution of marriage to hand, or mail, your spouse the stamped summons and petition and have that spouse return to you the signed and notarized Waiver of Service and Acknowledgment form for filing. Make sure ALL of the required documents are given to your spouse as required by your particular State Rules of Civil Procedure and any local administrative guidelines

What if you don't know where the other party is or how to locate them? Fear not, the legal community has thought of that. In Florida, if after a reasonable search to find the other party for service you are unsuccessful, then you are allowed to advertise your action in the local newspaper or post it on the court house bulletin board if you're indigent. There is a proper form for this. You must sign a due diligence affidavit stating that you have tried to find the other party for process of service but have failed. According to the Second District Court of Appeals of Florida, the test for a diligent search is "whether the complainant (petitioner) reasonably employed the knowledge at his command, made diligent inquiry and exerted an honest and conscientious effort appropriate to the circumstance to acquire the information necessary to enable him to effect personal service on the defendant". There is a standard due diligence affidavit in the Rules of Civil Procedure but the local administrative guidelines in my jurisdiction prefer a much more stringent affidavit. It is so stringent and ridiculous that nearly everyone including the lawyers and certain of the judges laugh at it. Not even God could answer it honestly. It would take a petitioner thousands of dollars and many months to generate the answers this local due diligence statement requires. Do you have letters from every military service affirming the party is not in the military service?...Do you have written confirmation from the United States Post Office, State Department of Motor Vehicles, County Voter Registration Office, Police Department, Sheriff Department, Highway Patrol, Florida Department of Law Enforcement, Federal Bureau of Investigation, Internal Revenue Service, the party's last employer, the party's family, the party's friends, and on and on and on and on, as to the known whereabouts of the party? Absolutely no one that we have heard of has honestly complied with this local due diligence guideline in our area. They just sign it and get on down the road with their action. That's right, the petitioners lie but I guess it makes the judges happy. What a joke!

A minor child was involved in this next example, Case No. DR 95-5014. A young working mother came to us for a dissolution of marriage. She could not afford the services of an attorney. She said she had phoned several lawyers but the least expensive was well beyond her reach. She had a year old child. She claimed her husband was on drugs and was abusive to her. All she wanted was out of the marriage and primary custody of the minor child. The parties had inconsequential marital assets. We informed her that her husband would have to pay child support as statutorily required by Florida law. The minimum amount of child support would be based on their respective incomes as plugged into the Child Support Guidelines Worksheet formula. We completed the appropriate paper work for her and she filed all the required documents at the court house. Subsequently, her husband was served by the Deputy Sheriff. To our surprise several days later she was served with a Summons and Petition for Dissolution of Marriage. Her husband had hired an attorney and also filed for a dissolution of marriage. I guess the attorney surmised that he could milk more money out of the husband if he filed divorce pleading instead of just an answer and counter-petition to the wife's original petition. The husband was requesting sole custody of the minor child among other things. The young mother went ballistic! She was scared to death and fully intimidated that she was going to lose her child. The most important thing in this young lady's life was her baby. We finally convinced her that in order for her to lose custody of her child, her husband and his attorney would have to prove that she was an unfit mother. And to prove that, they would practically have to prove that she was a prostitute, druggie or child abuser. She was none of these. In fact, she was really a nice hard working person that finally got fed up with a drinking, abusive spouse.

The wife filed a motion to dismiss her husband's petition. Since her husband's attorney failed to answer her petition in a timely manner (within twenty days of service), she filed a motion for default and was awarded the default by the Clerk of the Court. The husband's attorney also filed a motion to dismiss the wife's petition. Seeing that his incompetency was showing, the husband's attorney then filed a motion to consolidate actions. The attorney was in trouble and he knew it. It is interesting to note here that the judge refused to give the wife a hearing date on her motion but gave the attorney his requested hearing date for his motions. For each hearing this young lady had to take off from work while the attorney represented the husband. I guess the attorney had convinced the husband that the judge would make the wife pay all of the legal fees and costs.

I would like to reiterate that the parties here didn't have a proverbial pot to piss in nor a window to throw it out. In other words, they didn't eat $30 filet mignon every night. Nevertheless in the true "churn for more billable hours and excessive legal fees" fashion and as anticipated by me, the attorney filed interrogatories for the young mother to answer. It's voluminous but typical and I must share this with you:

INTERROGATORIES
1. EMPLOYMENT:
a. State the names and address of your present employer.
b. State the commencement of your present employment.
c. Describe your position or job.
d. State the names and addresses of your employers for the past three years.
e. If you are unemployed, state why you are not employed.

2. INCOME:

a. State your gross annual earned income, from all sources, for each of the last three years. Identify source and amount from each source.

b. State when you are paid and indicate for each pay period your gross salary and wages, itemize the deductions from your gross salary or wages and your net salary or wages.

c. Set forth any additional compensation, including, but not limited to, overtime, bonuses, profit sharing, insurance, expense account, automobile or automobile allowance, which you have received from your employer or anticipate receiving.

d. State your total annual income in each of the past three years.

e. Itemize all other income or support payments received.

3. ASSETS:

a. Describe by legal description and addresses all real property which you own, or in which you have an interest, setting for the percentage of your interest in each parcel. For each parcel, state date of purchase, purchase price and present market value.

b. List the names and addresses of all persons or entities which own an interest with you in the parcels of real property described in the foregoing sub-paragraph and describe such interest.

c. List all of the items of tangible personal property, including, but not limited to, motor vehicles, furniture, boats, jewelry or art objects which are owned by you or in which you have an interest. State your estimate of value for each item.

d. List the names and addresses of the persons who own an interest with you in the items of tangible personal property described in the foregoing sub-paragraphs and describe such interest.

e. List all accounts in which you have deposited money in your name or jointly with another person within the last 12 months.

f. As to the accounts set forth in the foregoing answer, set forth the account numbers, the cash balances and the persons and their addresses who are authorized to withdraw funds in said accounts.

g.   List all intangible personal property, including, but not limited to, stocks, bonds and mortgages owned by you or in which you have had an interest within the last two years. State percentage of your interest and the present value of such interest.

h.   List the names and addresses of persons or entities indebted to you and the nature and amount of their obligations to you.

i.   List all other assets which you own, have an interest in or the use and benefit of, setting forth your interest and value thereof.

j.   Describe in detail, including the cash value, all insurance policies of which you are the owner or beneficiary, including, but not limited to, health, disability and life insurance. As to each policy, list the issuing insurance company and policy number.

4. LIABILITIES:

a.   List all liabilities, debts and other obligations, indicating for each whether it is secured or unsecured, and, if secured, the nature of the security setting forth the payment schedule as to each and the name and address of each creditor.

b.   List all credit cards issued to you. Give the balance owed and present minimum monthly payment owed to each of such credit card companies and the account number for each account.

c.   As to each creditor, set forth the current status of your payment and total amount of arrearages, if any.

5. LIVING EXPENSES:

a.   Attach a completed Financial Statement, in accordance with Rule 1.611, Florida Rules of Civil Procedure.

b.   State the amount of money contributed monthly, directly or indirectly, for the support of any dependents for the past year next preceding the answers to these interrogatories.

6. MISCELLANEOUS:

a.   State your full name, current address, date of birth and social security number.

b. State the condition of your health and the name and address of all health care providers who have examined or treated you within the last 12 months. State the same information for your child.

I must admit I have seen longer interrogatories, especially when such assets as corporations and businesses are involved. But give me a break in this instance! The financial affidavit will more than cover this young mother's assets and liabilities. And no, she is not the CEO of IBM; she makes $7 an hour working for a title company. Anyway, her husband's attorney succeeded in intimidating the hell out of her in the court room. She was scared to death that her husband would get sole custody of her baby which was absolutely ridiculous. Her family pooled their resources and hired an attorney to accompany her to court. She still owes us $55 while the legal fraternity once again basks in its financial smorgasbord. I wish this young lady well as she and her child only deserve the best. Incidentally, even without a lawyer, I believe this wife would have easily been awarded primary custody of the minor child with child support coming from the husband as required by law.

I could write volumes on real life experiences with lawyers and judges in marital law situations. Most sound like fiction, but believe me they are non-fiction. I do not want to belabor the point but I do want to take the liberty of discussing a few more marital cases that just might give you enough insight to hold your own in pre-trial, trial or post-trial scenarios as a Pro Se Litigant.

Here is a case (Case No. 94-1095-FMDL) involving a problem with process of service. This was a dissolution of marriage case in Volusia County. We prepared all of the proper documents for the wife. She had minor children. She filed in the Volusia County court house in Deland. Wanting to expedite service of process on her husband, she hired an authorized, certified private process server to serve the petition and summons on her husband. The petitioner can usually save about a week by having a certified process server serve the other party versus having the local Sheriff do it. However, make sure the local administrative guidelines permit such service. Service on the wife's husband was accomplished and in twenty days' there being no answer or reply from the husband, a default was filed by the wife and entered into the record. Prior to hearing, the judge denied that service of process was valid. According to the judge, service by a certified private process server was not acceptable in his jurisdiction. The judge would only accept service by the Sheriff. I have heard of this no where else in Florida. Being a Pro Se Litigant who couldn't afford a lawyer, the wife really was not in a posture to appeal the judge's ruling to the District Court of Appeals. The remaining alternative was to file all of the documents once again and add the word AMENDED in front of each title with an alias Summons. Then request that the local Sheriff handle the process of service and pay for it once again. Having appeased this judge, everything else went smoothly. Knowing that Pro Se Litigants can't afford attorneys and don't know the legal process, judges will sometimes invent rules and procedures.

Sometimes having the other party served at his place of employment is more expeditious than service at his residence. But you have to realize that some large corporations will not let you serve them at work. Section 48.031(1)(b), Florida Statutes states, "Employers, when contacted by an individual authorized to make service of process, shall permit the authorized individual to make service on employees in a private area designated by the employer." In spite of this, often we have found in the central Florida area that the local sheriff will not confront such corporations as Lockheed-Martin, Westinghouse or Disney World in demanding service on one of these corporate employees on corporate property. In these cases we've had great success in service of process via a certified process server.

Here is one of my favorite cases. This fellow had been incarcerated a short period of time on an alleged white collar crime. He had gotten his life together and was working in outside construction. He and his wife had had a rather stormy, several year marriage. He still loved her and had financially taken care of her the best he could. Both parties recently moved to Florida. The wife hired an attorney and filed for divorce. They were in their late forties and had no minor children. They had a few assets but nothing to get excited about. Realizing that the husband was a Pro Se Litigant, the wife's attorney decided he was going to make a monumental case out of this action in an apparent attempt to make his house payments for the next year. The husband was not a doctoral candidate but he damn sure didn't fall off the turnip truck yesterday either. The husband was not the type to be easily intimidated. During his incarceration, he spent most of his free time in the law library educating himself. The wife's attorney really screwed up when he went after this Pro Se Litigant. The husband had a great sense of humor, and I really enjoyed working with this guy. After all of the preliminary legal mumbo jumbo of service, answer, counter-petition, various motions, etc., the husband wanted to let this lawyer know exactly where he stood. The husband was ready to bring all of this time consuming, legal fraternity fee enhancement to a head. A letter and a Pre-Trial Memorandum were formulated and sent to the wife's attorney. Incidentally, always mail the other party a copy of whatever you mail to their attorney as I know of cases where the attorney withheld pertinent documents from the knowledge of their client for a myriad of unsavory reasons. Let the client catch his attorney in a lie. Following are the letter and Pre-trial Memorandum. They were mailed out simultaneously. These documents will give you an idea on how to stand on your own two feet and not be intimidated by a lawyer. I have changed certain names and data in an effort to protect the innocent.

May nth, 19xx

Mr. Wife's Attorney
his address

Re: John Doe vs. Diane Doe, Case No. 93-0472, Twenty-fifth Judicial Circuit.

Dear Mr. Wife's Attorney:

I am in receipt of your PRE-TRIAL MEMORANDUM dated May x, 19xx. I have been informed that a pre-trial conference has been set for Wednesday, May xy, 19xx. I will be there.

Mr. Attorney, as you are aware, on May x, 19xx I mailed to your attention an Answer and Waiver and a Property Settlement Agreement. The settlement agreement was very similar to the one you had mailed to me previously for my signature. Your client failed to execute this document. Apparently we are starting to dance around with additional paperwork, motions, etc. Be advised, I am at a stage where there exists two possibilities in this action: either we are going to put this case to bed in a very short time or I am going to exercise my rights.

My wife and I were involved in a somewhat complex business/real estate venture in Michigan involving financial sums in the six figure range. To date I have been willing to forego incorporating that scenario into this action. I know my wife has not informed you about this and I advise you to ask her about it. I have numerous canceled checks, invoices, her hand written notes, etc. available for discovery and I will subpoena the same from her in an effort to document my allegations and subsequent requests of the court.

You should further know that in a protracted case I will subpoena as witnesses the following: about two dozen names are listed here and possibly others. My wife can inform you of their potential posture in this case.

Moreover, my wife's residency affidavit of being a Florida resident when she filed this petition is contradicted by the facts. I have evidence available for presentation to the court which will result in the granting of a Motion To Dismiss this case and you can start all over.

Further, on the yth day of May, 19xx, I filed a Petition For Rule To Show Cause on your behavior in several violations of the court orders. This behavior is continuing and will not be tolerated. I have not pushed for a hearing on this matter yet. Any ruling to deny me a hearing on this petition or a subsequent denial will necessitate my motion for a rehearing and/or possible appeal to the 5th DCA. Therefore, be advised that I have the deepest respect for the practice of law. However, the gratuitous barrage of legalize nonsense that you have authored (i.e. referring to me in your proposed settlement agreement as "herself" whereas I am a "himself") reflects the attitude that you have toward your art.

Insofar as the mobile home and recreational vehicle are concerned, I could care less which one I receive in the property settlement. I simply need a place to sleep and could care less which one the court awards me. Our other differences in the settlement agreement are inconsequential.

Mr. Attorney, should I not hear from you on or before, May xy, 19xx, I will assume we are in a full blown adversative position and will proceed accordingly. I trust your client has put down a large enough retainer to justify the time you may be about to charge this account.

Very truly yours,
John Doe
And now the Pre-Trial Memorandum that was mailed to the Wife and her attorney

PRE-TRIAL MEMORANDUM

The Husband, JOHN DOE, files his Pre-Trial Memorandum and states:

A. THE MARRIAGE:

1. Date and place of marriage - December xx. 19xx in Las Vegas , Nevada.

2. Date of separation - December xx, 19xx. However, Husband and Wife continued to cohabit occasionally thereafter.

3. Counseling - Husband requested counseling in his Answer And Counter-Petition to Wife's Petition For Dissolution Of Marriage (NOTE: Husband wanted to save the marriage if possible.)

B. THE CHILDREN:

1. None.

C. ALIMONY:

1. Neither party is requesting alimony.

D. REAL PROPERTY:

1.   ABC, Inc., a Michigan corporation owned jointly by Husband and Wife, has a promissory note in its favor in the amount of $50,000.00 executed the nth day of September, 19xx. The parties hereto as creditors are to receive $800.00 the first of each and every month beginning the nth day of October 19xx for 60 months and then a balloon balance is to be paid. Thus far, an estimated $16,000.00 plus interest has been paid to the parties hereto under this promissory note and Husband has not enjoyed any of the benefits of these payments to which he is legally due in a corporate function or individually. Husband requests an accounting and will proceed via discovery to ascertain the present status of this scenario.

2. Husband has contributed and deposited various large sums of money into the Wife's personal and corporate (ABC, Inc.) bank accounts taken from his other business ventures since his marriage to Wife and hereby demands an accounting of those funds.

E. PERSONAL PROPERTY:

Suggested Disposition

1. MOBILE HOME. The parties are owners as tenants by the entireties of a two bedroom Rott Kinde framed mobile home which is presently located at zzzzzzzzzzzzzz. The Wife should transfer her interest in the mobile home to the Husband. After transfer of full ownership of the mobile home to the Husband, he agrees to assume full responsibility for the payments on the mobile home, and to indemnify and hold the Wife harmless therefrom.

2.   DIVISION OF PROPERTY. The Husband shall receive the contents of the marital residence above.

3.   19xx Ford. The 19xx Ford presently titled in the Wife's name shall be her sole and exclusive property. Wife agrees that she shall be fully responsible for any and all debt, liabilities, responsibilities and obligations associated with said vehicle and shall defend and hold the Husband harmless. The Wife further agrees that should the

Husband incur any liabilities or costs or expenses associated with said vehicle or should anyone take any legal action against the Husband in connection with this vehicle, she will fully reimburse the Husband for any and all said costs, including reasonable attorney's fees and costs.

    4. 19xx SCOUT MOTOR HOME. The 19xx Scout Motor Home presently titled in the Wife's name shall be her sole and exclusive property. Wife agrees that she shall be fully responsible for any and all debt, liabilities, responsibilities and obligations associated with said vehicle and shall defend and hold the Husband harmless. The Wife further agrees that should the Husband incur any liabilities or costs or expenses associated with said vehicle or should anyone take any legal action against the Husband in connection with this vehicle, she will fully reimburse the Husband for any and all said costs, including reasonable attorney's fees and costs.

    5. 19xx CHEVROLET. The 19xx Chevrolet presently titled in the Husband's name shall be his sole and exclusive property. Husband agrees that he shall be fully responsible for any and all debt, liabilities, responsibilities and obligations associated with said vehicle and shall defend and hold the Wife harmless. The Husband further agrees that should the Wife incur any liabilities or costs or expenses associated with said vehicle or should anyone take any legal action against the Wife in connection with this vehicle, he will fully reimburse the Wife for any and all said costs, including reasonable attorney's fees and costs.

F. DEBTS AND SUGGESTED DISPOSITION OF DEBTS.

    1. Each party shall be responsible for any and all debts he or she incurred in his or her separate name prior to, during or subsequent to the marriage between the parties, excepting that the Husband will responsible for those debts owing to Kane Furniture Co., Inc. and MasterCard 12345689 only.

G. ATTORNEYS FEES AND COURT COSTS.

    1. Wife shall be responsible for Husband's attorney's fees and costs.

H. TRIAL EXHIBITS.

1. Promissory Note...XYZ, Inc., a Michigan corporation, to ABC, Inc., a Michigan corporation.

2. ABC, Inc., a Michigan corporation, incorporation documents.

3. Copy of various deposit slips showing Husband's monetary deposits into ABC, Inc. checking account.

4. Copy of various canceled checks of Husband's used to pay debts of Wife.

5. Copy of various handwritten notes by Wife relevant to financial status et al.

6. All bank records of Husband and Wife.

7. Copies of cashier checks in Husband's name, deposited in Wife personal and business accounts.

8. Copies of receipts for labor and materials paid for by Husband for improvements and renovations to the bar/restaurant business/residence in Michigan in excess of $60,000.00.

9. Copy of security agreement and promissory note dated September nth, 19xx giving a security interest to the Husband in regards to the property described in Item 1 above in the amount of $101,000.00.

10. Copies of transcripts from the kkkkkkkk County Court, State of Michigan, regarding a previous civil action brought by the Wife against her former husband and requesting alimony because of her inability to operate the above described bar/restaurant, and her indebtedness to her present Husband in excess of $39,000.00 for equipment purchases, materials, subcontractor labor, and repairs to the above described bat/restaurant/residence, business and corporation.

11. Copies of Wife's hand written notes used by her for sworn testimony in the above action.

12. Copy of the court order from the Circuit Court of kkkkkkkk County, Michigan, granting alimony requested as a result of the above testimony by the Wife.

13. Copies of the Internal Revenue Service tax records and State of Michigan tax records, both personal and corporate, stating the Wife's indebtedness to her present Husband for cash loans made to the Wife and her corporation.

14. Copies of canceled checks of the Husband's company account showing expenditures to relocate Wife from Tttttttttttt, Michigan to Rrrrrrrr, Michigan in excess of $6,100.00.

15. Copies of canceled checks of the Husband's company account showing expenditures in excess of $58,000.00 for equipment and material purchases for the renovation of the business and residence described above.

16. Receipts for materials, subcontractor labor, equipment, furnishings, etc. describing the aforementioned renovations and labors.

17. Copy of Husband's Builders License issued by the State of Michigan showing Husband's vocation prior to and during his relationship with Wife.

18. Copy of Husband's current credit report showing Husband's credit is at its limit as a result of expenditures on Wife's behalf and of her family.

19. Copies of real estate documents showing Husband owned and sold four (4) parcels of real property during his thirty (30) month relationship with Wife, realizing actual profits in excess of $95,000.00 cash.

20. Copies of bank records that show only the Wife enjoyed a profit in excess of $41,778.98, deposited in her corporate account after expenses of the sale of the aforementioned business and property.

I. MISCELLANEOUS:

1. Request for amendment of Pleadings: Yes.

2. Necessity for further discovery: Yes. As regards ABC< Inc., a Michigan corporation, etc.
request of standard marital interrogatories of Wife.

3. List of pending motions: Yes. Petition For Rule To Show Cause. Motion For Continuance.

I HEREBY CERTIFY that a true and correct copy of the foregoing has been furnished by U. S. Mail this nth day of May nth, 19xx to: Wife's Attorney et al.

JOHN DOE, Husband/Pro Se Litigant

We had worked hard on the Pre-Trial Memorandum and the letter but it paid off. Copies were sent to not only the wife's attorney and the wife but the court. The attorney immediately backed off. No more jerkin' around with superfluous motions and paper work from the wife's attorney. Everything was resolved and the final judgment awarded within thirty days! The Husband estimated he saved between $10,000.00 and $15,000.00 in legal fees and probably a year or two in time by representing himself.

I think it's obvious that the Husband still carried a torch for the Wife. He had really let her run over him financially during their several years of married life. Anyway, he finally awoke to realization and decided to get on with his life.

In another case, the wife divorced her husband three years ago. He just wanted out and agreed to everything the wife wanted. The husband had no lawyer representing him in this action. He was a stockbroker at the time, making decent money. The parties had three minor children, the oldest of which was 15 years old. Subsequent to the divorce, the husband lost his job and took a tremendous pay cut. For the past year his monthly net take home pay after child support was deducted was $153!! Needless to say, he fell behind on child support. Here is another of a multitude of cases where the husband could not afford an attorney and he did not know he needed to file a petition to modify child support for it not to accumulate as arrearages. He came to me and I prepared a Petition for Modification of Child Support along with interrogatories for the ex-wife to fill out pursuant to Florida law. At about the same time, the ex-wife filed a Motion for Contempt for non-payment of child support and a hearing date. The ex-wife refused to obey the discovery laws and give us her financial affidavit plus other requested financial documents. We needed these documents in order to ascertain what the new child support amount should be. In Florida it is a legislatively mandated formula to find out what the minimum amount of child support should be. We prepared a Motion to Compel and Motion for Continuance on the ex-wife's contempt motion. With our motions our client filed the appropriate orders for the judge to execute plus self-addressed, stamped envelopes for the orders to be mailed out to the parties. The judges and their judicial assistants are so damn lazy that they rarely will write a simple order and then mail it out to the parties on their own initiative. Our hearing occurred before the ex-wife's contempt hearing. Judge AD granted the continuance and told the ex-wife to honor the discovery rules and give the ex-husband the documents he requested or he would find her in contempt. However, the judge refused to sign the order to compel or the order for continuance and just let it ride. The ex-wife gave us another financial affidavit and nothing else. Then she got a quick hearing on the contempt motion once again. The ex-husband explained to Judge AD that the ex-wife had not complied with the Court's recent orders. Additionally, he told Judge AD that there was a great disparagement between the financial affidavits given 37 days apart by the ex-wife and therefore, they were highly suspect. Judge AD said he didn't care and the ex-husband had four days to pay the $3,000 in back child support or go to jail. Judge AD said the ex-husband should get a lawyer. The judge didn't give a damn about the pending petition to lower child support or the fact that the ex-husband had been unemployed through no fault of his own. The ex-husband was forced to sell his only means of transportation, a pickup truck worth about $7,000, for $3,000 in order to pay the back child support and keep out of jail.

I reviewed an interesting cite from the 5th District Court of Appeals (Fla. L. Weekly D500). This was an action involving a dissolution of marriage in which the husband appealed the trial court's (circuit court} decision. The parties stipulated that the husband earned $15,000 monthly. Of this amount, the court awarded the wife "$6,000 a month alimony, $1,656.58 per month to cover the income tax on the alimony, $1,292.80 per month to cover the cost of an insurance policy on the husband's life naming the wife as beneficiary, and $1,386.00 per month as child support. This totals $10,335.38 as monthly support or over two-third's of the [husband's] income." Based on Section 61.30, Florida Statutes child support guidelines, the child support statutorily required came to $735.54 per month, nearly half of what the $1,386.00 child support the Court ordered. If the husband still has to pay federal taxes on his monthly income which I am sure he will, this guy will probably leave the country in order to be able to survive. Incidentally, the 5th DCA affirmed the lower court's (circuit court) decision here and obviously really didn't give a damn whether the husband could survive or not.

I would like to mention here that quite often women are financially devastated as a result of divorce. According to federal statistics, 22% of divorced female retirees live in poverty and the situation is expected to get worse. Golden years look bleak for divorcees.[58] Especially when the husband's pension plan is challenged during a divorce wherein the wife is entitled to half of the plan does the lack of legal knowledge and a non-cooperating pension plan administrator hurt the spouse. Even when women have won retirement benefits, they do not know how to get them unless they hire an attorney. In most instances, the legal fees for the lawyer are too great to warrant help in the pension matter. It really makes you want to cry.

<hr>

[58] USA TODAY 8/8/2000

CHILD SUPPORT AND CUSTODY

Child support and custody are going to be discussed together. In many instances a modification of custody usually involves a modification of child support. There are a number of reasons a petition for modification of child support and custody can be justified. Only the most common and basic reasons will be discussed here.

When filing a petition to modify a court order, the petitioner must put the other party on notice. The Florida courts have said that a petition involving a modification of a previous court order in marital law doesn't necessitate service of process by a Sheriff or certified process server as it is an ongoing action. Certified mail, return receipt is usually sufficient. However, in an effort not to start any problems with a judge who thinks he knows it all, I would strongly advise having the other party served by the local Sheriff or process server. It'll be worth the extra $20 - $30 service fee. The typical documents involved in a child support and/or child custody modification include Summons, Certificate of Service, Memorandum of Service to Sheriff, Petition, Uniform Child Custody Jurisdiction Affidavit (UCCJA), Financial Affidavits, Child Support Guidelines Worksheet, Notice To Payer, Income Deduction Order, Order and any other petty documents required by the local administrative guidelines. Some jurisdictions require your petition to be called a Supplement Petition For Modification of Final Judgment or Petition For Modification Of Child Support And Child Custody or Motion To Modify Child Support and Custody or whatever. Remember, the Supreme Court says it's the subject matter and not the form that counts in the documents you file as a Pro Se Litigant. Just try to convince some old, crusty local judge of that fact....

In a way, child support modification is similar to alimony modification; there must be a significant change in income of either or both parties from the time the original order was executed to warrant a modification of child support. Some judges believe a minimum change of 15% is required but believe me, it is absolutely up to the discretion of the presiding judge.

Like the dissolution of marriage (divorce) scenario, one's income is ascertained via financial affidavits, income tax returns and possibly interrogatories. The same Rules of Civil Procedure apply. If you are the petitioner and the other party refuses to cooperate, file a Motion to Compel. Most of the actions and terms I am discussing have been defined and discussed elsewhere in this book. If you are the petitioner and your former wife has remarried and is living a life of luxury with the your kids in their new environment and you are busting your ass to make child support payments on time, it may be time to act. In this instance, definitely send interrogatories to the ex-wife. The interrogatories should include such questions as, does your husband pay the house mortgage payments, utility bills, telephone bill, your vehicle mortgage payment, credit card invoices, food bills, vacation costs, your and the minor children's personal clothing bills and if so, specifically how much and exactly what items. Ask if the aforementioned moneys expended by her husband are his personal funds and if not, whose are they. Ask where and when she went on vacations since the rendering of your final judgment and who paid for them and who went. Ask what is the market value of the home in which she and the kids live. Ask what her husband's job and income are. Ask what current assets she owns by herself and jointly. The questions that you can ask in an interrogatory are only limited by your imagination. Be advised though, you can only ask a maximum of thirty questions. Refer to your State Rules of Civil Procedure. Legally the income and assets of the ex-wife's husband should not be considered in a modification of child support. But it blows the average judge's mind if the new husband is some dude making in the six figures, living in a million dollar home while you're living in a $300 a month apartment, making $900 a month and paying $500 a month child support. The judge is not supposed to deviate more than 5% from the minimum child support as legislated in Florida. But remember, the judge thinks he is God and if a party doesn't like his decision, they can appeal it The judge can do any damn thing he wants to in that court room and don't you ever forget it. And if his golfing buddy is your ex-wife's attorney, you've really got a problem!

In Florida child support also takes into consideration health insurance for the minor children. It is supposed to be reasonably available in order for the paying spouse to be ordered to pay for it. Life insurance on the party paying child support to cover the support payments should the demise of the payer occur before the minor children no longer are eligible for child support is to be considered. The bottom line here is that the discretion of the presiding judge dictates the insurance scenario.

Case No. DR-91-10961 involved an ex-husband who came to us for help in lowering his monthly child support payments. I won't belabor the point of how he tried to get a lawyer to represent him but the cost was beyond his reach. We agreed to help him for the total cost of $125. He couldn't believe it.

Back in 1991 this fellow's wife hired an attorney and filed for divorce. The husband couldn't afford an attorney to represent him. As is typical he did not know the legal procedures or how to represent himself as a Pro Se Litigant. Nor did he realize that an independent paralegal could offer substantial aid to him at a very reasonable cost. The husband did not answer the summons and petition for dissolution of marriage he was served in a timely manner (20 days). A default was entered. The husband did not even file the requested financial affidavit with the court. He did nothing to defend himself. This is a lawyer's dream. In the final judgment the judge imputed the husband's income. In other words a determination by the judge was ascertained as to the amount of child support the husband should pay. The imputed amount of child support was significantly higher than what the husband was actually earning. The judge ordered the husband to pay $721 per month child support and honored the attorney's request for the husband to pay alimony to the wife, also. The lump sum support alimony ordered was $5,0000 to be paid at the rate of $50 per month.

Husband and wife were both gainfully employed with each earning approximately $1,200 monthly. In addition, the husband was ordered to pay the wife's attorney fees and other incidentals. Now you know where the saying, "Gettin' shafted" comes from. The judge could have cared less about the husband. The judge was probably more concerned about being on time for his luncheon date with Sally Mae.

This poor, ex-husband was having one hell of a time trying to make the child support and alimony payments. He had no idea that what the judge had ordered was illegal. One of his cohorts suggested he file for a modification. The husband found out about us and we formulated a Petition For Modification of Child Support And Alimony with all appropriate ancillary documents for him. Deleting the caption, notarization paragraph and certificate of service notation, the body of the petition looked somewhat like this:

PETITION FOR MODIFICATION OF CHILD SUPPORT AND ALIMONY

Petitioner/former husband, JOHN DOE (SSN 123-45-678), moves to modify the previously entered Order for child support and alimony and as a basis therefor says:

1. The Final Judgment of this court entered on the nth day of June, 19xx, included as a part thereof the following:

"B. That there were two (2) minor children born of the marriage, to wit: etc., etc. etc.

9. That the Husband shall pay the sum of $721.00 per month as and for child support...."

2. Since the entry of the Final Judgment, former husband and former wife have had a significant change in financial status as exhibited by their respective, current financial affidavits.

3. Based on child support guidelines in Section 61.30, Florida Statutes, the imputed figures from the former husband's and former wife's current financial affidavits show the former husband is paying in excess of the child support guidelines as dictated by statute. This is causing the former husband to suffer undue financial hardship.

4. The Final Judgment of this court entered on the nth day of June, 19xx, included as a part thereof the following:

"11. That the Wife is hereby awarded lump sum alimony in the amount of $5,000.00 for her support and said sum shall be paid in installments of no less than $50.00 per month beginning July 1, 19xx, and shall continue the first day of each month thereafter until paid in full."

5. The former wife currently receives child support and alimony from the former husband and she now enjoys secure employment with a governmental entity where her income and benefits are in excess of that of the former husband.

6. Former husband, JOHN DOE, resides at ZZZZZZZZZZZZZZZZZ. Former wife, SALLY MAE, resides at YYYYYYYYYYYYYYYYYY.

WHEREFORE, the former husband respectfully moves the Court for an order decreasing monthly child support payments from $721.00 per month to that sum as required pursuant to Section 61.30, Florida Statutes or that sum the Court deems just and proper. Additionally, the former husband respectfully moves the Court for an order totally ceasing any and all alimony payments to former wife.

Dated this _____ day of _____, 19xx.

_____
JOHN DOE, Former Husband/Petitioner

The former wife hired an attorney to represent her in this petition. Her attorney started with the normal stream of interrogatories, motions, etc., anything to accumulate billable hours to justify the attorney's fees. In the husband's dealings with this attorney we found out that she, the attorney, was really exceptionally nasty. I've got to show you the Motion To Dismiss the attorney filed. Talk about a piece of nebulous garbage. The attorney got a hearing date for her Motion To Dismiss subject petition (more billable hours) and the husband represented himself as a Pro Se Litigant.

MOTION TO DISMISS

COMES NOW the Former Wife, SALLY MAE, by and through the undersigned attorney and files this Motion to Dismiss the Former Husband's Petition for Modification of Child Support and Alimony dated March nth, 19xx, and as grounds would show:

1. That there is no legal basis for the court to modify, alter, or change an award of lump sum alimony.

2. That as to the Former Husband's request that the child support be reduced, an analysis of the Former Husband's current and past financial circumstances fail to show a significant change in circumstances and therefore the Former Husband fails to state a cause of action.

3. That at the time of the entry of the Final Judgment of Dissolution of Marriage, although the Former Husband had not filed a financial affidavit, the court made a determination for the purposes of calculating the Former Husband's obligation to pay child support that his net monthly income was $1,271.71.

4. That according to the Former Husband's financial affidavit which was signed but not dated yet filed with the court on March yth, 19xx, the Former Husband's current net monthly income for the purposes of determining his child support obligation is $1,187.00.

5. That the difference in the Former Husband's income is not sufficient to justify a reduction in child support obligation.

6. That the Former Husband has failed to allege any circumstances which could give rise to a modification of the Former Husband's child support obligation.

7. That the Former Wife has retained the undersigned attorney to represent her in this cause and is obligated to pay reasonable attorney's fees and costs and the Husband is well able to pay same.

WHEREFORE, the Former Wife respectfully prays that the Court dismiss the Petition For Modification of Child Support And Alimony, award to the Former Wife attorney's fees and costs and grant such other and further relief as may be just, proper and appropriate.

I HEREBY CERTIFY that a true and correct copy etc., etc., etc..........

_____

MONEY GRABBER, ESQ., Attorney for Wife

At the hearing the judge denied the attorney's Motion To Dismiss. From that moment on the wife's attorney because very easy to deal with. After that it was a slam dunk for the former husband. He paid us in full.

Let's review a couple of child support cases that are somewhat similar in nature. Both former husbands were uneducated, neither having graduated from high school. They did not have, nor could they afford, legal representation during their respective dissolutions of marriage. Neither knew what the hell happened to them in court other than they were ordered to pay child support and their wives' attorney fees. Neither had a vocational discipline but worked manual labor when they could find it. They were not boozers, druggies, criminals or on welfare. These guys just weren't very smart and, therefore, prime bait for financial milking by the legal fraternity. Like one lawyer told me, "They may not be able to pay the fee in one lump sum, but boy do I ever have a lot of annuities being paid to me monthly! Ha-Ha" Typical lawyer...

Case No. DR-91-3200 and we'll call the former husband JOE BLOW. Joe has had a hell of time trying to pay his child support. His former wife had her attorney file Motions for Contempt against the husband in the past for late and non-payment of child support. Joe was told to come see us. We scrutinized all of his paper work relative to this action. The court (judge) had violated the law by incarcerating Joe for contempt without the proper determinations of his "ability to pay". Joe

77

had no attorney to defend him and he didn't know a damn thing about the rules of civil procedure or any other substantive rules for that matter, so why the hell should the judge care about this poor, pro se litigant? He didn't. We put together a Petition For Modification of Child Support for Joe with all ancillary required documents. The caption is omitted in the following petition:

PETITION FOR MODIFICATION OF CHILD SUPPORT

Petitioner/former husband, JOE BLOW (SST 123-45-678), moves to modify the previously entered Order for child support and as a basis therefor says:

1. The Final Judgment of this court entered on the nth day of May, 19xx, included as a part thereof the following:

5. Child Support Payments: Commencing June yth, 19xx, the Husband shall make child support payments to the Wife in the sum of $340.00 per month for the child, until the child reaches the age of 18 years, dies, marries or becomes self-supporting...."

2. Subsequent to the aforementioned Final Judgment, former Husband has been adjudged in contempt of the Court's order to pay child support and was incarcerated. Significant involuntary changes in the former Husband's financial environment have made it virtually impossible for the former Husband to honor this Court's order for payment of child support. This Court was in error to incarcerate former Husband for "willful" contempt of this Court's order to pay child support. This Court was in error to incarcerate former Husband for contempt for contempt for violating this Court's order to pay child support without first determining the ability of the former Husband to pay said child support. Edwards v. Sanders, 622 So. 2d 587 (Fla. 1st DCA 1993); Mourra v. Mourra, 622 So. 2d 1359 (Fla. 5th DCA 1993). "[W]hether the contemnor has the *present* ability to comply (with court order to pay child support) before incarceration is ordered" (emphasis added). Scapin v. Scapin, 547 So. 2d 1012, 1014 (Fla 1st DCA 1989). According to the Florida Supreme Court in Bowen v. Bowen, 471 So. 2d 1274 (Fla. 1985), the present ability of the contemnor to pay means the contemnor must have actual resources, cash or assets, in which to

purge himself. "[I]f a civil contemnor is without any assets or cash to pay the purge amount, a trial court can not jail him for civil contempt." Scapin at 320.

Additionally' former Husband is entitled to a hearing to demonstrate that he does not have the ability to pay arrearages of child support. Cook v. Navarro, 611 So. 2d 47 (Fla. 4th DCA 1992). The so-called "hearing" conducted on September nth, 19xx by a Judicial Hearing Officer in this instance is considered highly suspect at best by the former Husband.

3. Since the entry of the Final Judgment, former Husband has had an involuntary, significant decline in financial status. Former Husband's financial affidavit shows he has no assets and at the present time he is unemployed and receiving AFDC in the amount of $241.00 per month.

4. Based on child support guidelines in Section 61.30, Florida Statutes, and assuming the former Wife has no income, the former Husband's previously reported $350 per month income is less than the lowest stipulated "combined monthly available income" of $500 per month which designates a "minimum child support amount" of $48 *per month* for one child.

5. By extrapolation from the data given in paragraph 3 above, former Husband's minimum child support payment should be $30 *per month*. Since former Husband has been borrowing money to meet everyday living expenses, child support payments in excess of $30 per month at this time would not only put an undue financial hardship and burden on former Husband but it would be impossible for former Husband to obey such a directive of this Court.

6. Former Husband resides at *ZZZZZZZZZZZZZZ*. Former Wife resides at XXXXX.

WHEREFORE, the former Husband respectfully moves the Court for an order decreasing monthly child support payments from $335 per month to not more than $30 per month child support and decreasing child support arrearage payments from $10 per week to $20 per month to be paid to the former Wife by the former Husband or that sum the Court deems just and proper.

Dated this _____ day of _____, 19xx.

_____

JOE BLOW, Petitioner/Pro Se Litigant

Remember that your petition should be notarized and include the Certificate of Service paragraph certifying a copy went to the adversarial attorney (or other party). Any and all documents which you file with the court should be copied to the other party.

Shortly after filing the above petition, the former husband had us put together a petition for modification of visitation, also. His ex-wife was even refusing to let him see his child. Reference to the former Husband's visitation rights in the final judgment was great for the ex-wife but left him hanging. This is a basic format to consider for petitions to modify child visitation:

PETITION FOR MODIFICATION OF CHILD VISITATION

Petitioner/former Husband, JOE BLOW (SST 123-45-6789), moves to modify the previously entered order for parental responsibility and as a basis therefore says:

1. The Final Judgment of this court on the nth day of May, 19xx, included as a part thereof the following:

"4.   PARENTAL RESPONSIBILITY.   Parental responsibility for the minor child shall be placed solely with the wife, subject to the Husband's rights of reasonable contact with and access to the minor child upon reasonable notice....   The child shall spend Father's Day and the Husband's birthday with the Husband. The child shall spend Mother's Day and the Wife's birthday with the Wife."

2. Wording of the Final Judgment is so nebulous so as to afford former Wife opportunity to withhold minor child visitation rights from former Husband at former Wife's discretion subject only to Father's

Day and former Husband's birthday. Accordingly, former Wife has denied former Husband of certain of his visitation rights.

3. The best interests of the minor child are not being served under those visitation rights as given in the Final Judgment. The minor child is being denied the normal requirements needed of a young minor female with an ongoing family relationship with her biological father.

WHEREFORE, the former Husband respectfully moves the Court for an order modifying parental responsibility (visitation) as stated in the Final Judgment so that the minor child may visit with her biological father every other weekend from 7:00 P.M. Friday until 5:00 P.M. the following Sunday, Father's Day and former Husband's birthday from 9:00 A.M. until 5:00 P.M., every other Christmas Day beginning 19xx from 9:00 A.M. until 7:00 P.M., and any 3 hours between 5:00 P.M. and 10:00 P.M. on the minor's birthday or those visitation rights the Court deems just and proper.

Dated this _____ day of _____, 19xx.

_____
JOE BLOW, Petitioner/Former Husband

Whenever you file a pleading, petition, modification or whatever with the court and you are asking for some sort of ruling, always include a prepared order affirming your request so all the judge has to do is sign it. The other side does this. Always read the order which was authored by the other side and if you don't agree with the wording, file a motion saying so. Even if the judge has already signed the order, you have 10 days to file an objection with the court. Following is an example of an order which this former husband filed. The story behind this order was that due to certain overt and despicably discriminatory actions by the presiding judge against the former husband, he filed a Motion for Recusal (disqualification). Being a good Pro Se Litigant, he filed the order with the motion. Here is what the order looks like in Florida:

Legal Whores

IN THE CIRCUIT COURT OF THE THIRTIETH JUDICIAL
CIRCUIT, IN AND FOR XXXXXX COUNTY, FLORIDA

IN RE: The Marriage of
JOE BLOW,   CASE NO. DR-91-3201
          Petitioner/Former Husband.
and
SALLY BLOW,
          Respondent/Former Wife.
_____/

ORDER ON MOTION FOR DISQUALIFICATION OF JUDGE

THIS CAUSE came on for hearing this date on the former Husband's motion, and it is hereby,

ORDERED AND ADJUDGED that the undersigned Circuit Judge, having found that former Husband has filed a legally sufficient motion under Fla. R. Civ. P. 1.432, does hereby disqualify himself in this case and directs the Clerk of the Court to reassign said case to another division of the Court by blind rotation.

DONE AND ORDERED in Chambers, YYYYYYY County, Florida, this _____ day of _____, 19xx.

_____
I. M. INCOMPETENT, Circuit Judge

copies to:

          Joe Blow   Sally Blow
          address   address

Incidentally, the former husband, Joe Blow, got his new judge who honored his requests in modifying the child support and visitation. He wasn't financially able to pay us for our efforts in helping him but he did compensate us by fixing the broken office lawn sprinkler system and maintaining the office landscape for a period of time.

CASE N O. 81-413-CA is very similar to the above case so I won't go into as much detail. The ex-wife divorced the husband some dozen years ago. He had no attorney then nor now. This poor dude was making a valiant effort to pay the court ordered child support but was backing up instead of making any progress in catching up. The fellow not only was uneducated, he could hardly communicate in the English language. I'd say he was in his middle fifties and really looked like he had just come off skid row in Chicago. He said he heard about us and he did not want to go back to jail due to unpaid child support. He obviously couldn't afford a lawyer and had enough common sense to realize that the legal fraternity didn't care about him. His ex-wife had her attorney file another motion for contempt with the court for his non-payment of child support. In the past couple of years, these motions for contempt filed by the ex-wife have resulted in the presiding judge incarcerating him in the county jail for 60 consecutive days each time. The venue was in north Florida, Clay County. Same situation as the Joe Blow scenario just above, except this fellow did not want to modify his court ordered child support. He just wanted to respond to the contempt charge and not be incarcerated again.. The judge didn't give a damn about the law, ability to pay, judicial ethics, or anything else, knowing this pro se litigant couldn't afford an attorney or an appeal. The former husband was in arrears over $4,000 in past child support and his wife's attorney fees, had court ordered child support payments of $129 per month, and he was currently making between $150 and $400 a month when he could find a job. He didn't even have a federal tax return to refer to in order to affirm his financial plight because he really didn't think you had to file a return if you made less than $10,000 a year!

I formulated Former Husband's Response To Former Wife's Motion For Contempt With Memorandum Of Law document and drove him the 125 miles to the hearing in Clay County. He had no transportation. I sat in the back of the court room watching this same obnoxious judge that had put this guy in jail twice before on his ex-wife's "willful" contempt charges. Not being a member of the Florida Bar I could not represent the former husband in court but I could sit in the back and watch. At the previous hearings for contempt, the former husband just stood there in front of the judge with no attorney and not knowing how to defend himself. Each time the judge had sentenced him to 60 days in the county jail even though this guy did not have the "ability to pay" as required by law. I had made up my mind that if this judge sentenced the fellow again, there would be an appeal to the district court of appeals and a formal complaint made to the Judicial Qualifications Committee about the judge's conduct. The judge saw me come into the court room with the former husband and sit in the back. The judge started the hearing and took time to read the former husband's motion in its entirety. The judge looked to the back of the court room where I was sitting and then dismissed the former wife's motion for contempt and told the former husband to get out of his court. On the way out this fellow was nearly in tears when he thanked me profusely for helping him and saying, "It is really wonderful not leaving this courthouse and going directly to jail and I am very thankful." Hell, I got choked up. We charged him a total of $45 on this one. Subsequently, we were successful in an action lowering the child support for this fellow.

I would like to interject a comment here. A competent independent paralegal can make a living in this vocation if they can fend off the brutal attempts by the legal fraternity to intimidate them. I am not a knight in shining armor nor am I trying to save the world. We do charge folks for our services...sometimes. Our intent is not to make a profit nor is it to lose money.

Case No. 85-3890-CA-19-P is a unique child support and custody case that warrants telling. It gives you an excellent view as to how screwed up and bureaucratic our legal system is. The father was never married to the mother but admitted paternity at the birth of the minor child He had been paying court ordered child support to the biological mother from the child's birth. The mother was the primary custodial parent. The father had visitation rights which he faithfully exercised. The mother suddenly died and the minor child, now a teenager, moved in with the father. Child support payments had been made through an income deduction order to the father's employer. The child support was automatically deducted from the father's pay and mailed to the Clerk of the Court for disbursement to the mother. Following the death of the mother, the father took the mother's death certificate to the Clerk of the Court in an effort to cease the child support payments. The Clerk's office denied his request and told him to hire an attorney. The least expensive lawyer the father could find to help resolve this problem wanted an immediate $600 retainer and told the father he could probably get the child support deductions stopped in several months. The attorney told the father that a petition would also be required requesting of the court that child custody be modified to give the father custody of the minor child. Total cost would probably run around $1,200 to $2,000. The father was referred to us by a previous client. We quoted him a total cost of $145 which he paid up front. We guaranteed him stoppage of the child support deductions. We informed him he would get reimbursement of any child support payments deducted from his pay since the mother's death and also any support payments which the Clerk had which had not been disbursed to the mother. In the same petition to the court, we quoted the applicable statute and requested a change of custody to the father due to the circumstances. This gave the judge something to hang his hat on and he immediately signed the order. In less than 30 days and for $145 we made one father a very happy fellow.

Recently a young man phoned us about his on-going non-contested divorce. He and his wife hired an attorney to do the paper work. They had no assets to speak of, a few liabilities and one minor child. They had agreed on everything. They questioned the attorney about how he had constructed the property settlement agreement and more particularly about whose responsibility it was for paying certain bills. The husband had agreed to pay specific liabilities which erroneously were shown in the agreement written by the lawyer to be the responsibility of the wife. The attorney informed them not to worry because the child support the husband would be paying to the wife would cover these bills. I told this husband that he needed to find competent legal advise because if this attorney told him the above, he was unequivocally incorrect. The young man said he had asked another lawyer and an independent paralegal about the using of child support moneys for the purpose of paying off bills as explained by his attorney in the property settlement agreement. Both said absolutely no way. He asked that we finish the paper work for his dissolution of marriage. We completed the balance of documents he needed and charged him $95. When I asked the husband how much he and his wife had paid the attorney, he declined to answer saying he was too embarrassed to tell me. Not only do you have to worry about being financially raped by the legal fraternity, but how do you know if they are competent?

Case No. 93-518 involved an acquaintance of mine who was a cook at a restaurant. This fellow I'll call Max had two children by a woman, his wife, who left him during the marriage to live with his buddy. They lived in another state. Subsequent to the divorce, Max was paying court ordered child support. His English is atrocious and he really can not comprehend the legal system or his court ordered responsibilities. Unemployed for about a year he got behind on child support, was petitioned by the State and at the hearing was incarcerated by the court. He could not afford an attorney since he was unemployed. He had no idea what the hell was going on and ended up in jail for 30 days. He had no concept of his being able to halt child support until he was employed again since the child support kept accruing. Now this guy was not a dead-beat in that he truly loves his children and was actively trying to secure employment. His first incarceration lasted 30 days. He was able to borrow $3,000 from family members to get out of jail. The law says you must have the ability to pay your child support and/or arrearages in order to be incarcerated for non-payment. If you don't have the ability to pay, the law says the court can not jail you. The law very specifically says you must not be forced to borrow moneys in an effort to stay out of jail. What a joke! I know for a fact that Max didn't have a "pot to piss in or a window to throw it out". Max received a subpoena from the Florida Dept. of Revenue saying he was behind in child support and must come to a hearing with his financial affidavit. I helped him get a copy of the computer print out from the Clerk of the Court here and from New York (the original jurisdiction) which showed his child support payments. The local print-out erroneously did not show payments he had recently made to the tune of $3,500. The printout from New York showed that these payments had been made to the New York child support agency. You see, Max had moved a couple of times between New York and Florida and got confused as where to make his child support payments. Luckily he had the canceled checks for the payments in question which he had made to New York. We mailed copies of these canceled checks to the local Florida DOR child support enforcement agency along with a letter explaining what had occurred. They didn't really give a damn and told Max he had better attend the scheduled hearing for non-payment of child support. I went to the hearing with Max acting in the capacity of an interpreter. There was a court reporter, General Master acting as judge and a skinny girl acting as attorney for the Dept. of Revenue (DOR) in the hearing room. Max's ex-wife and two children were still living in New York and were not at this hearing. After making us wait for 3 hours they began the hearing The General Master let the DOR attorney run the entire proceeding. They did not give a damn about Max's canceled checks nor the computer print-out from New York which showed Max had erroneously made the child support payments to New York instead of Florida. It didn't matter to the DOR attorney that the support moneys in question already had been disbursed to the ex-wife as child support. The DOR attorney said the New York print-out was not certified and that was that! She accepted only the Florida computer print-out although it was not certified. Max's financial affidavit showed he had about $2,500 net assets (old car, some worn out furniture and used clothing). The DOR attorney realized Max was not a rocket scientist and raked him over the coals. Not being an attorney, I could not come to his defense. She totally intimidated Max and made him admit additional assets which I knew damn well were not there. When Max told her that he had purchased $4,000 worth of furniture some 6 years ago, the DOR attorney put it down on the financial sheet as having a current market value of $4,000. This was totally wrong as the present value of the asset is what is supposed to be entered. If Max could have gotten $500 for what he called furniture, it would have been a surprise. Max showed her where he was now working and an income deduction order was taking the $490 a month child support directly out of his $1,330 monthly income. But the DOR attorney demanded that Max be incarcerated unless he could pay $5,800 in arrearages right then and there. Max couldn't come up with that amount of money in 6 months if his life depended on it and the attorney knew it. Luckily, the General Master gave Max some slack. The hearing was rescheduled for the next morning They opened the hearing by asking Max if he had the $5,800 with him and he said no. They then illegally put handcuffs on Max as a precursor to being incarcerated. Max was frantic in that he had a great fear of going to jail again. He literally begged to let him call some family and friends in an effort to borrow the money. The General Master agreed after the DOR attorney said it was okay. Before the morning was over, Max was able to borrow $5,800 to give to the Court in order not to be incarcerated for non-payment of child support, most of which he had already previously paid through the New York courts...a totally illegal action by this court! The judicial system just doesn't give a damn. This is not a rare occurrence. If the poor bastards can't afford an attorney, then screw'em. The system knows if these pro se litigants can't afford an attorney, they damn sure can't afford to appeal illegal orders to the appellate court.

In this case there were two egregious violations of law committed by the court. Firstly, in a cause such as this, one must have the ability to pay court ordered child support before being incarcerated. It was plainly obvious that Max did not have such ability. Secondly, a General Master does not have the authority by law or statute to incarcerate anyone. However, it's done nearly every day. The judiciary tries to get around this accusation by saying the General Master's report and recommendation are approved by the judge immediately after any hearing; it is called INSTANTER ORDER. But this is baloney! The defendant, like Max in this case, is immediately handcuffed and taken off to jail under the General Master's orders. The judge may not approve and execute the General Master's report and recommendation for days or even weeks! This deprives the defendant his constitutional rights and reverts us right back to the days of the British colonial empire here in America. But then again, the judiciary in this country truly don't give a damn if you can not cough up enough money to employ one of these greasy slim-ball attorneys to represent you in court.

Interestingly enough, as I was writing the lurid story above, some 2 weeks later the Florida Law Weekly published a decision from the Florida Supreme Court (24 Fla. L. Weekly S78) about child support enforcement. The case[59] deals with the improper incarceration of a father pursuant to child support arrearages without proper determination of present ability to pay purge amount. Reading this case will really piss you off if you are not an attorney or judge. The opinion is too voluminous to copy here but I would urge you to get a copy of it and read it in its entirety. It exemplifies and adds credibility to my story on Max above. The Supreme Court finally acknowledges the wrongdoing in these instances and I quote, "We recognize that our decision today will impose the requirement of additional hearings on an already heavily burdened judicial system. However, inconvenience cannot be cited as a reason to deny an individual the due process to which the individual is entitled. Incarceration to obtain compliance with a court order may indeed be warranted when a contemnor has the ability to comply with the order and willfully refuses to do so, but incarceration for the simple failure to pay a debt is clearly prohibited. We will not allow our rules to be modified to serve as the basis for creating a debtor's prison." The irony of this opinion is that the circuit courts and their administrative staffs in general will ignore this opinion and continue with business as usual. The average slob that can not afford an attorney will continue to get screwed by the judicial fraternity. Hello, world...is anybody out there?

Here is where a Pro Se Litigant went to trial in a custody case. The petitioner had become a father while not married to the minor child's mother. The father admitted paternity and had been faithfully paying court ordered child support for the past nine years. The child's mother had custody and was the residential parent. In the interim the father married, but not to the child's mother, and subsequently had 2 children of the marriage. The initial child's mother never got married

---

[59] Anthony Gregory v. Everett Rice, Sheriff of Pinellas County, Florida

and remained single. The father and his new wife were very concerned about the "best interests of the minor child" of the father. The father could document that the child had several instances of head lice while living with the mother. He could prove that when the child's school had made numerous attempts to contact the unmarried mother they could never get her. He had irrefutable proof that the child just was not receiving proper care at home. The father finally hired an attorney to initiate a custody proceeding in an effort to get custody of his little girl. After the attorney bled the father for a substantial amount of money, the attorney dropped the case. The father was now back at "square one" less the funds the lawyer sucked out of him. The father and his wife came to me for advice. Since the child's mother had an attorney and the father only had a third grade education and could barely read, I informed him that going against the attorney in a trial atmosphere would be tantamount to suicidal. Even if all of the law, God, the President and the Governor were on the father's side, he would stand absolutely no chance of winning custody in a trial as the lawyer would eat him alive via judicial procedural maneuvers. His strong feelings for the best interests of his little girl were so intense that the father said he had to live with himself and must try something, even if he had to go it alone. I agreed to help him.

He filed a Petition For Modification of Child Custody which I prepared. I would estimate that the father spent upwards of 40 to 50 hours in preparing for the trial. The child's mother had previously admitted to the father in private that she really did not care about the child but did not want to give up the child support she was receiving from the father. The mother's attorney began his barrage of time consuming legal mumbo jumbo via the rules of discovery with interrogatories, etc. The father earns about $16,000 a year and owns a small house and has 4 dependents. His assets are meager in the best case scenario. All the discovery generated by the attorney gains nothing but additional legal fees for the lawyer in this scenario. The petition for custody filed by the father contained about 35 pages of documentation from school personnel and doctors, affirming that the child had some serious mental and physical problems. From the nature of the reports one did not have to be a psychiatrist to ascertain that the root cause of the little girl's problems was her mother and the environment in which the child was living. Incidentally, the mother worked at a local honky-tonk and took the little girl there with her during working hours. As procedurally required at the pre-trial conference the father submitted the names of witnesses and documents which he anticipated using at the trial. Subpoenas were issued and served by the sheriff. A trial date was set.

The father's wife was well educated and along with me helped the father organize a good, strong presentation for the judge. Even though he could not read very well, with his wife at his side directing him, the father believed he could make a decent presentation to the court. Without her at his side, his presentation was really dead in the water. I informed him that there was a good possibility that the judge would not permit his wife to help him because she was not a party to the case and was not an attorney. He felt justice would prevail and the judge would permit his wife to be next to him at the trial under the circumstances. Sure....

The trial begins. First thing out of the box is the judge asking who is sitting next to the father/petitioner. Upon finding out that the father's wife is not a party to the action nor an attorney, the judge orders the wife to sit out in the gallery. The father's attempt to convince the judge that his wife was an integral part of his presentation fell on deaf ears. Since he could not read his opening statement, the father verbally stumbled along until he called his first and only witness. The other witness he had subpoenaed failed to show up. The father's intent with this witness from the school system where his little girl attended was to prove the mother's negligence. Starting with the first question to the witness from the father, the attorney objected on a procedural basis. The judge sustained the objection, i.e. agreed with the attorney. This action repeated it self for the next 5 or 6 questions until the frustrated father gave up. The father then turned to the judge and explained in his own words the love and concern he has for his daughter and the wrongs being perpetrated upon her by the mother. He respectfully asked the judge for custody of the child. The judge asked if he was finished and then acknowledged it was time for the lawyer to present his side. The lawyer requested a directed verdict saying that the father did not prove his case and therefore should be denied here and now. The judge concurred and denied the father his petition for custody. What a great country this is with true justice and equity!!! Give me a break... I told the father he would have to borrow, steal, rob or get another job to get the money to hire some greedy lawyer to take his case. He reminded me that he had already been that route and would not go to another lawyer. The poor fellow was beside himself and equally frustrated. From my expertise and experience I knew that the father had a solid case for getting custody of his daughter.

I knew a young lawyer that owed me a big favor. I contacted this lawyer and told him I was ready to pick up my "I owe you". He took the case for $500. I had already prepared all of the paperwork. We got a hearing and with this attorney won the custody case in about 30 minutes! Yes sir...true justice! All you have to do is pay the judicial fraternity in order to get results.

PATERNITY

Establishing the biological parenthood of a minor is called paternity. This action is usually necessitated when a child is born out of wedlock. Paternity bestows certain legal responsibilities upon the biological father such as child support and similar ancillary factors. Paternity can be contested or non-contested.

In a non-contested paternity action the procedure is very simple. Forms for paternity have been dispensed to the public by the Florida Supreme Court. These forms can be used in both contested and non-contested paternity suits. The simplicity of this action brings me to a recent occurrence I must share with you. A young, unmarried couple came to me for help in a paternity situation. The young man's name was on the birth certificate of the 3 year old minor child, and he had been paying child support since it's birth in excess of that required by state statute. The parties were not living together but wanted to establish legal paternity. Both agreed on all matters, including child support, visitation, parental responsibility and custody. They thought they had to hire lawyers and each employed their own lawyer some 20 months ago. Firstly, these blood sucking lawyers got a temporary paternity order for child support through the court. Then after more nebulous motions and wasted time, the lawyers finally put together a stipulation agreement for the couple which was supposed to lead up to a final paternity order. This young couple were not rocket scientists but they did have enough brains to finally realize these attorneys were just sucking thousands of dollars out of them as legal fees in a giant churning of legal fee action. They fired their attorneys and came to me. I wrapped up their case in less than hour and charged them $25. The court executed the paternity order I had written and everyone is happy. Incidentally, the couple individually filed complaints with the Florida Bar against these two attorneys even though I assured them no disciplinary action would be taken against the attorneys.

The main purpose in a paternity action is to legitimize the minor child and to legally dictate child support, visitation and custody. If non-contested, the birth certificate which displays the father's name in conjunction with the appropriately filled out Petition For Paternity and ancillary documents should suffice for the court hearing and subsequent paternity order. The child support in Florida usually will be set pursuant to Section 61.13, Florida Statutes. Visitation, parental responsibility and custody are negotiable and are decided by the parties with the concurrence of the court. No attorneys are needed...nor desired.

Contested paternity requires a scientific test to ascertain whether or not the father is in fact the biological father of the minor child. These tests typically include blood or DNA procedures. The results are accepted by the courts. The forms for Petition for Paternity are used here also. However, certain available additional paternity forms may be required in light of the requirement for the scientific testing. No attorneys are needed here either. If you have any questions, phone your nearest paralegal first. You'll generally get a straight answer at no cost rather than paying some lawyer for some verbal quagmire of needless information which usually turns out to be of no value to you whatsoever.

Men need to be very careful when involved in a paternity action, regardless of their intent. It is very commendable owning up to being a father and wanting to fulfill all of the responsibilities of being a father, including child support. I have known of men who paid child support in cash sums of money before being ordered to do so by the courts. Over the years some of these men paid significant cash sums to the minor child's mother and had no canceled checks or other proof of having paid child support. The child's mother would then file a paternity suit requesting child support from the day the child was born. The court would order the father to pay this back child support known as arrearages even though he had already paid it once before. He had no proof! It happens. Believe me, I've seen it. Remember, it is a court of law, not a court of justice.

I recently turned down an interesting paternity case. A gentleman was the defendant in a paternity case where the mother of the minor child wanted 17 years back child support. Paternity had never been established and the man's name was not on the birth certificate. The mother filed the paternity action alleging the man as the biological father and requesting scientific testing. The man was served via U.S. Mail. He didn't reply. He was served twice more and never responded. He still did not reply or answer the complaint. The mother's attorney filed a motion for default and the court rendered a default judgment. The court awarded the mother $33,000 in back child support and an income deduction order to have the moneys taken from the man's paycheck. The man swears he is not the biological father but it is too late; too late for the court to even permit him to take a scientific test to prove his innocence. He let the time go by in which he could file a timely appeal and the local jurisdiction has denied his request to vacate the judgment. He might have an outside chance in overturning this judgment on a due process constitutional basis due to questionable service of process. On that premise I advised him to seek the legal counsel of a competent attorney. His legal fees most certainly could surpass the owed $33,000 in attacking the given circumstances on a constitutional basis in the appellate courts. Which goes to show you, answer complaints and summons in a timely manner when you are served. Even if you use a pencil and scribble on a piece of scrap paper, file it with the court and it is considered an answer and the courts can not issue a default on you.

Paternity issues can get complex but in the vast majority of paternity cases a lawyer is not needed. Save your money.

As an adjunct action in a paternity case, the majority of times visitation of the minor child by the non-custodial parent is never addressed at the hearing. It should be. I guess this is so that the non-custodial parent has to end up hiring some sleazbag attorney to pursue visitation rights. In fact, just the other day a lady phoned me on just this cause. Paternity had already been established some months previous and now the father acting as a pro se had filed a petition for visitation.

The father wanted the mother to bring the minor child to the father's mother's house in another county some distance away for a period of 7 hours once a week. The petition said the mother could wait at this residence until the 7 hours were over. Under the given conditions I do not believe any judge, well, nearly any judge in his right mind would grant such a request. The lady was beside herself and hired a lawyer that charged her $1,500. There was a hearing in front of a General Master and the father won. The father had no lawyer. Following the hearing the lawyer told the lady, "Sorry, but that's the way the Court rules." She asked my advice. Firstly, I informed her that she could file an "Exception" within 10 days of the rendering of the Recommendation of the General Master in which she would be heard on his issue by a circuit judge. She told me that her lawyer never told her about an "Exception". I surmised that the idiot attorney probably didn't even know what an "Exception" was in marital law in Florida. I counseled the lady best I could over the phone and wished her luck. She was not too hapy when I told her I did paternity visitation petitions for $175 and guaranteed our work. In this instance I would have guaranteed the lady she would not have to take the child out of county for visitation and wait around for 7 hours under the given conditions. Had the judge ruled accordingly, this would have been another free appeal by me to the District Court of Appeals for abuse of judicial discretion against the circuit judge.

Incidentally, the 20 minute hearing and the 15 minutes it took to prepare for the hearing with the answer to the petition with some nominal additional time to go to the restroom, netted this attorney an estimated excess of $500 per hour. This lady was furious but had no basis to retaliate against this lawyer. The legal fraternity would cover this boy's butt in a myriad of ways.

ADOPTION/CUSTODY/GUARDIANSHIP

Adoption of a minor child can be a very complicated legal issue. It is a financial boom for attorneys. Even rare adoptions of adults by adults can be legally vexing. Most states require a member of the Bar to represent clients in adoption cases. However, this is not true in Florida in step-parent adoptions. Usually a husband desires to legally adopt his wife's child that is not his biological child. There could be many reasons for this action but I only want to bring to light a couple of possible repercussions at this time. Once a child is adopted, the individual adopting the child has the same legal responsibilities bestowed upon him as if the child were his biological child, including but not limited to child support and inheritance. The biological father (in this example) is then off the hook for child support, etc.

The procedures and forms for step-parent adoption are usually very simple and straight forward. The services of an attorney are not needed. The Florida Supreme Court has approved forms for this very action. If the biological father were to contest this action and hire a lawyer, you would be well advised to hire a lawyer yourself. However, if the biological father consents or says nothing or can not be located, you can easily go it alone without an attorney. The most expeditious way is for the biological father to give his written consent. The forms are self-explanatory and easy to complete. Any paralegal can guide you straight, efficiently and economically.

Just last month I had a young lady come into my office requesting the cost of a step-parent adoption and the amount of time it would take. I quoted her $225 plus the filing fee and said it would probably take 4 weeks. She thought I didn't understand what she wanted and asked that I repeat my answer. On finally realizing what my fee was and the time allocation, she informed me that her attorney wanted $6,000 for the same thing and told her it would take 6 to 9 months. I questioned her further to insure there were no hidden hookers relative to her case. It was a simple stepparent adoption which was finalized by the court in less than 4 weeks. The lady and her husband love me! Initially the lady was very apprehensive due to the great disparity in the charges between me and the attorney. I assured her that the paper work was the same and the extra $5,775 the lawyer was charging her would be for holding her hand in the court room for the 30 seconds they would be in front of the judge.

Our paralegal office does a significant number of step-parent adoptions. We do them efficiently, economically and expeditiously. In fact, we have been known to take over step-parent adoptions wherein the hired attorney has screwed them up, financially soaked the people, and incurred the loss of a great deal of time for the lawyer's ill prepared endeavors.

Custody of minor children is discussed in depth in the chapter on DIVORCE but will be touched on here in a somewhat different manner. Sometimes there comes a need for family members to take over the legal responsibility of the minor children from the biological parents. By family members I mean aunts, uncles, brothers, sister, grandparents, etc. A formal guardianship or custody action can accomplish this need. However, the law mandates the services of an attorney in a guardianship action. Also, an attorney can be necessitated in a custody proceeding depending on the specific circumstances. Either way, the attorney fees are mind boggling. The best way around this is to file a Petition For Temporary Custody By Extended Family in Florida. You accomplish the same purpose, quicker and a hell of a lot less expensive The state statute pursuant to this cause is simple and leads you through what is required in the petition. Any paralegal should be able to help you with this course of action. Once again, consent by the biological parents for this temporary custody, although not necessary, helps expedite the action.

You should be able to visit your local law library at the court house, public library or institution of higher learning to peruse through

98

the necessary law books for the course of action to take in your particular jurisdiction. This is exactly what the young lawyers do who have just passed the Bar exam and just started practicing law.

FLASH!!!   It has just been brought to my attention that the Florida Bar has succeeded in getting the Florida legislature to pass new laws regarding stepparent adoptions. It seems that now one has to file a Petition for Termination of Parent Rights before filing for an adoption. And with this petition one must file a Declaratory Judgment. No sooner than 30 days after filing these documents, you must then file the stepparent forms previously mentioned in this chapter. This is nothing more than a redundant action. But now one must hire an attorney for the simple stepparent adoption. So the simple $225 adoption will increase to the many thousand dollar route in another successful effort by the lawyers to grease their pockets.

Legal Whores

GENERAL AND SPECIAL MASTERS

In the rush for attorneys to make huge sums of money in the legal industry, it is imperative that the courts help them funnel as many litigants as possible in as short a period of time as possible through the legal morass. In an effort to accomplish this feat the courts have established a unique system. The courts have initiated another layer of legal bureaucracy for the litigant, mainly in the domestic relations portion of law. This additional layer is called the General Master or the Special Master. This system accomplishes two things. Firstly, it tends to lighten the circuit judges' trial load. Secondly, it provides a political pay-off plum for paid appointment to the status of a General Master for some lawyer who can't survive financially in the open market as a lawyer.

Court hearings in marital law (domestic relations) involving temporary child support, temporary alimony, motions for contempt and other mundane actions are now being relegated to the General Master. The majority of the hearings before the General (Special) Master in Florida are by pro se litigants, those poor slobs that can't afford an attorney to represent them and the courts are reluctant to screw around with them but have to because the U. S. Constitution says so. The parties to a General Master hearing have the right to cancel said hearing and request to be heard by a judge instead. On request by either party the hearing will then go before a judge. None of the pro se litigants are aware of this option and end up being the result of a legal "kangaroo court". The pro se litigant can file an "exception" with any result of the General Master hearing within 10 days of being served with the General Master's Report and Recommendation and the judge must then hear

101

the case. Once again, the typical pro se litigants are not aware of this option and continue to be at the mercy of the General Master.

Historically, General Masters treat pro se litigants like scum and with great disdain. I guess the General Master gets a joy and thrill out of embarrassing and/or incarcerating someone who is not educated, whose income is considered at the poverty level or who is not represented by an attorney. I have never been able to figure this out. Maybe it's a power thing... Anyway, the General Master's report and recommendation are taken before a judge sometime after the hearing (from a couple of hours to a couple of weeks) and the judge 99.99999% of the time just signs it to make it an official order. In cases involving back child support, the General Master usually has the Respondent, the one who owes back child support, jailed immediately after the hearing if payment is not forthcoming right then and there. This action is totally and unequivocally illegal. Yet they do it on a daily basis and are doing it today. It had gotten so bad the Florida Supreme Court in its decision Gregory v. Rice[60] ordered that this process cease immediately. But guess what...it continues to go on today. The General Master does not have the legal authority to incarcerate anyone without a judge's executed order. But who cares? The pro se litigant slob without legal representation is ripe for another legal fraternity screw job.

I would like to briefly discuss the Gregory v. Rice case. In this case the father was sentenced to 90 days in jail with a $200 purge even though the unrefuted record established that he had no money and no assets. After the presentation of testimony, a hearing officer (General Master) found that the father "had been or was employed for six months" even though the testimony clearly established that such was not true. The General Master recommended incarceration and the father was then immediately incarcerated without a proper determination that he had the ability to pay according to a procedure used in Pinellas County, Florida whereby a circuit judge signs the General Master's order without review of the record.

---

[60] 24 FLW S78 (Fla. 1999)

The Florida Supreme Court was appalled at the overwhelming violations of one's constitutional rights when appearing before General Masters. This Court laid down specific and finite rules and procedures to be followed by the General Masters in their hearings. The irony of it all is that nothing has changed: the General Masters still conduct business as usual as though the Supreme Court never made this decision. Who really cares and who is going to hire some lawyer for thousands of dollars and complain via the court system? Nobody!

In the Gregory v. Rice cite the Florida Supreme Court states, "Additionally...we concluded that prior to imposing any sanction, particularly when the sanction is incarceration, the hearing officer (General Master) must advise the alleged contemnor (poor slob) of the alleged contemnor's rights under this rule. As noted, under Rule 12.491, any party may file a motion to vacate an order within ten days from the date the order is entered and any party may move to modify the order at any time (e.g. Exceptions). Because many contemnors have no counsel (lawyer) and may be unaware of their rights under this rule, it is imperative that officers advise them of those rights. Otherwise, contemnors may sit in jail for extended periods of time without realizing they had the right to contest the order or have it modified". Yea...right... What a joke! The Supreme Court continued, saying, "We recognize that our decision today will impose the requirement of additional hearings on an already heavily burdened judicial system. However, inconvenience cannot be cited as a reason to deny an individual the due process to which the individual is entitled." What a crock of horse manure! The General Masters continue to "deny the individual the due process to which the individual is entitled" to this day. While casually discussing this matter with a circuit judge recently, I was told that the above scenario was just tough crap on the individual or pro se litigant and that they should have an attorney representing them in the first place to protect their due process rights.

I wish the press or media could be present at some of these General Master hearings and expose what is going on. That will never happen as the General Master clears the court room of all except the parties and their lawyers, if they have one. Also present is usually a secretary and the Assistant State Attorney acting as a prosecutor. This

Assistant State Attorney is similar to the General Master in that he or she is a lawyer working for the State because he or she usually can't make a living on their own in the private sector of law. The typical Assistant Attorney has a chip on their shoulder and could care less that they are violating the law in the manner of questioning or asking for evidence from the parties in the action. Hell, there are no witnesses and besides, who knows to challenge them if you don't have legal counsel representing you. Talk about a genuine kangaroo court. I was able to get first hand knowledge on what really goes on in these hearings by acting as an interpreter during certain hearings and also by interviewing literally hundreds of my clients following their hearings before the General Master. It is unbelievable what goes on in these hearings. Can you believe the General Master will illegally incarcerate a person right at the hearing for non-payment of back child support without a court order and without ascertaining that they have the ability to pay? It happens every day.

I believe a person should be jailed for contempt when they are not paying court ordered child support. However, there are certain finite requisites which must be adhered to before incarcerating anyone in this country. In Florida, the law states you must have the "ability to pay" child support and refuse to pay in order to be incarcerated. The General Master does not give a damn whether or not you have the ability to pay...off you go to jail. Just last week I saw a case in front of the General Master where a father proved without a doubt that he had sold what furniture, tools, machinery, automobile, and other personal property that he had in order to try and pay his child support but was still behind. This fellow had a take home pay of $1,240 monthly and a monthly child support obligation of $700 for two children. He had been trying to get a second job but to no avail. He was still $750 behind in child support. You guessed it. The General Master had him immediately jailed for contempt on non-payment of back child support. I found out that this fellow subsequently lost his job because he was in jail. The only way he can get out of jail is to purge out, that is, pay up the back child support. Now where in hell is this fellow going to get the money to get out? Borrow the money? Even if this guy could borrow the money to purge himself, the law very specifically says one should not have to borrow funds to pay purge amounts to get out of jail. All of these actions are direct violations of the U. S. Constitution and the Bill of Rights.

The above example is just one minuscule example of how the General Masters are violating folk's constitutional rights and the laws of the land. I assume it will never cease as who really gives a damn about the ignorant, underpaid jerk that can't afford a lawyer.

I must relate another General Master story that recently occurred. A pleasant lady came to me for a divorce. She had three children and had been literally kicked out of the marital residence by her husband. She and the children were now residing with her mother in a small apartment. This lady was employed by the school board in a common labor type employment. Needless to say, her resources were quite limited. Her husband had a good job and was apparently stable. I agreed to help her and told her to ask the Courts to make her husband pay for all fees and costs. In an effort to get some money flowing to this mother who was in dire need of assistance I helped expedite her case. The paperwork was completed and filed within 2 days. The husband was served the summons and petition by the Sheriff within 4 days and a hearing was set for the lady before the General Master for temporary child support and temporary alimony within 6 days. I never had experienced a case move so expeditiously before and it made me feel good as the lady was very appreciative of my efforts.

All legal points and requirements had been met when the lady appeared before the General Master pro se by herself. The General Master in this instance was an attorney that couldn't make a living on the outside as a lawyer on her own. She gave the lady hell for not having a lawyer represent her and told her she could do nothing for the lady until her husband was served the original petition for dissolution of marriage. The lady told her he had been served but when the lady could not produce the affidavit of service the General Master concluded the hearing and ran the lady out of the hearing room. She immediately came to my office with the above story. I was furious! I asked her if the General Master had opened her file which was before the General Master and she replied no. Then I suggested that the lady return to the court house and request to see her file and check to see if the affidavit of service was in the file. If it was there I told her to go back to the General Master and demand a hearing. Yes, she found the affidavit of service in her file and demanded a hearing. The General Master's secretary gave the lady a hearing in one month.

The shame of this whole scenario is that due to the General Master's arrogance and laziness of not even opening the lady's file and noting the affidavit of service, is that the lady must go another month without temporary child support and alimony to help her get by financially. Do you really think the General Master or the legal system gives a rat's ass about this poor mother and her children who can't afford to hire a lawyer? Give me a break!

There are literally thousands and thousands of stories where the Court system (General Masters, clerks, secretaries, etc.) treat Pro Se Litigants like lower class citizens. I really wish I could print these stories here but that is impossible. The only true justice in our legal system is dictated by money.

STATE ATTORNEY/ LOCAL LAW
ENFORCEMENT/PROSECUTOR

The State Attorney and local law enforcement agencies can be known as prosecuting attorney and police or sheriff, respectively in your locale. One group arrests and the other tries to get a conviction in the courts. Both usually are self-serving whose main concerns are numbers and statistics, with the State Attorney being the worst of the two. They must generate acceptable numbers insofar as arrests and/or convictions are concerned. Whether you are guilty or not has little, if any, relevancy whatsoever in compiling these numbers. Multitudes of arrests and convictions look great in one's jacket file and when running for re-election.

I do not intend to go into great length about this subject here. Suffice to say, if you get arrested do not say a word to the arresting agency. Call a criminal lawyer immediately. (And I have no great love for lawyers.) Do this especially if you are as innocent as the newly fallen snow. Even if you are not guilty of the alleged crime, you can incriminate yourself and not even know it and I don't care how brilliant you think you are. The Jon Benet Ramsey murder case in Boulder, Colorado is a good example of folks covering their butts. Jon Benet's parents refused to talk to the local authorities without their attorney. They were smart. The local state attorney wants an arrest and subsequent conviction: he doesn't give a damn whether or not they are guilty. He just wants the opportunity to convince a jury the Ramsey's are the guilty party. And we all know how intelligent juries are; remember the O. J. Simpson jury? Sure, I strongly support the concept that the bad guys belong in prison. But the good guys don't. The record reflects that too many folks have been incarcerated and subsequently proven innocent.

The USA TODAY[61] published an excellent typical example of the point I am trying to make. A man was arrested by the local cops before the Jacksonville Jaguars - Tampa Bay Buccaneers football game November 15th for selling two $34.72 tickets for $35 apiece, 3 cents above the profit limit. The cops and prosecutors were foaming at the mouth wanting to convict this criminal and put him away where he belongs...in prison. "He broke the letter of the law", said Assistant State Attorney David Barksdale.[62]   Incidentally, during the arrest the cops took $216 from this guy plus he missed a great game. The city fathers in their albeit late infinite wisdom rescinded the ordinance and let the guy go.

The recent innovation of DNA testing has initiated release of a significant number of convicted felons in that they were scientifically proven not to be the guilty party. They are the lucky ones. What about the poor innocent dudes where DNA testing or other credible evidence has no bearing? Since the modern death penalty was instituted in this country in 1973 over 80 men and women - one for every seven executed - have been released from death row because they were wrongfully convicted.[63] Florida alone accounted for 18 of these exonerations from the death penalty. I won't go into detail here of the myriad of examples where these wrongly convicted individuals spent years and years incarcerated until they were found innocent via DNA testing. This data and stories would consummate an entire book by itself.[64] Some states have executed people with credible evidence of innocence because their claims were raised too late or had other technical glitches. If proven innocent folks are put to death, what in the hell do you think happens to

---

[61] December 29, 1998

[62] Orlando Sentinel 11/26/98

[63] New York Times 5/23/99

[64] New York Times 8/20/00, 10/8/00: USA TODAY 9/13/00, 9/11/00, 10/2/00

people who are wrongfully convicted of lesser offenses and subsequently found to be innocent? If they don't have a ton of money for a defense or some powerful person or organization takes up their cause, as we say in Mississippi, "they are shit outa luck." The point here is, all law violators should suffer the penalty established by law but just because you really are innocent, doesn't mean you won't be found guilty. An excellent example that readily comes to mind is the case of Roy Criner of Texas who spent a decade on death row for conviction of rape and murder.[65] It nearly took an act of Congress to get the Courts and prosecutors to let his lawyers introduce DNA samples proving his innocence for a new trial. Most of the time the Courts refuse to admit new evidence in a capital conviction even though it would exonerate the defendant. The legal fraternity's attitude is that the verdict is in and it must be right, don't bother us.

Another example of prosecutors going ballistic is the recent federal case where the feds arrested Los Alamos scientist Wen Ho Lee and incarcerated him for over 9 months while they played games with his case in the media and federal courts. Dr. Lee allegedly violated classified laws by downloading some of his work into his computer. It was tantamount to jaywalking but the federal prosecutors made a big case out of it. The director of the FBI had committed a much more serious similar offense by downloading classified material into his laptop computer and losing the damn thing in a taxi or wherever: he doesn't remember. Yet was he prosecuted? Hell no! The federal prosecutors were salivating over the prospect of getting some good media attention for themselves in the Dr. Lee case. To hell with Dr. Lee who had devoted himself, his entire life to helping maintain the United States as the No. 1 super power in the world with his nuclear works and impeccable work record. The whole scenario was such an obvious travesty of justice that Federal Judge James A. Parker stunned a suddenly hushed courtroom by implicitly singling out Attorney General Janet Reno, Energy Secretary Bill Richardson and senior officials in the Clinton White House for what he said was a questionable indictment,

---

[65] USA TODAY 8/16/2000

for misleading him about Dr. Lee's supposedly deceptive behavior and then for ignoring his urges that the government ease the "demeaning, unnecessary punitive conditions" under which Dr. Lee was being held. Judge Parker then publicly apologized to Dr. Lee on behalf of the U.S. federal government.[66] The USA TODAY[67] in their editorial aptly stated, "Rather than overreaching in this weak case, prosecutors should have kept their powder dry for a strong one." Poor Dr. Lee, a man known for his knowledge and integrity, had to spend thousands and thousands of dollars for lawyers to defend him. No, he ate the costs of his defense, no reimbursement.

The USA TODAY[68] newspaper had an excellent commentary on "Panel cites abuses in federal grand juries". According to a panel of the National Association of Criminal Defense Attorneys there are few checks on the power of federal grand juries, resulting in a system that allows prosecutors to indict whomever they wish. "The balance has shifted so dramatically in favor of the prosecution that it has been noted, time and again, that a good prosecutor could get a grand jury to indict a ham sandwich." Don't believe it? Just ask Dr. Lee above.

Again, there are thousand s of stories like the ones above, but I really don't wish to belabor this point here.

---

[66] New York Time (/14/00

[67] 9/12/2000

[68] July 5, 2000

APPEALS

There are various layers of jurisdictions in the court system in our respective states and country. In Florida, for example, the court system begins with the county court followed in chronological order by the circuit court, district court of appeals, and finally the Florida Supreme Court. I will use the Florida court system as examples in this discussion. Your particular state may vary slightly in nomenclature and procedure. This primer will not discuss the appellate procedure involving the federal courts as that subject is much too broad.

If the presiding judge in your case in county court rules against you and you feel he is legally wrong, you have the right to appeal to the next higher court. In this instance, the next higher court would be the circuit court. If so desired, you can then appeal the circuit court's decision to the district court of appeals. If your case was initiated in the circuit court, you would direct your appeal to the district court of appeals of which there are five in the State of Florida. To appeal the district court of appeals decision to the Florida Supreme Court or federal courts your action must be based on violation of your constitutional rights or possibly certain other limited causes. One can petition the Florida Supreme Court or federal courts but there are certain stringent and procedural requirements that are beyond the scope of this book. Appellate procedures in the Supreme Court or federal courts should not normally be your concern as a Pro Se Litigant.

There is a rule of thumb in the legal industry regarding appeals. It is said that one in twenty-five lower court decisions appealed to the district court of appeals is reversed while one in a hundred appeals directed to the Florida Supreme Court is reversed. On that basis, you have a 4% chance of success in the district court of appeals and a 1% chance with the Florida Supreme Court.

In giving a decision on an appeal, the court usually returns the decision as AFFIRMED, DENIED, and/or REMANDED. The appellate court may return any one or combination of these rulings in its decision. AFFIRMED means the lower court's ruling stands and is sanctioned. DENIED means the lower court's ruling is reversed. REMAND means the lower court's ruling is being sent back to the lower court with instructions from the appellate court for additional hearings, decisions, etc. The appellate court can affirm part of a lower court ruling, deny part of it and/or remand part of the same ruling.

The appellate courts always have the option of giving a written opinion and the reasons (basis) for their decision or a simple one word AFFIRMED or DENIED ruling. A written opinion is appealable to the next higher court if it meets certain criteria. A one word ruling, e.g. AFFIRMED (Per Curium Affirmed...PCA), is usually not appealable and, therefore, is the final say. You will have reached a dead end in the judicial system in that action with no other readily available legal recourse. The reason I think this one word opinion is ludicrous is because it gives the appellate court an easy out in those appeals where they do not want to publicly muddy the water or make waves. An excellent example is a Pro Se Litigant appealing a marital law decision of the circuit court to the district court of appeals. From my experience, this Pro Se Litigant has tantamount to one chance in a million of getting a favorable written opinion (lower court ruling REVERSED) from the appellate court. The vast majority of the time the Pro Se Litigant will receive a one word AFFIRMED or PCA (lower court ruling approved) decision regardless of the validity of his claim. I believe the main reason for this is if the appellate court were to rule favorably for the Pro Se Litigant in this, the largest segment of actions and causes in the court system today (marital/family law), the appellate courts would be inundated with appeals from Pro Se Litigants. With Pro Se Litigants representing themselves on the appellate level, you'd have thousands of lawyers not receiving these potential huge legal fees. Don't be so naive to believe that law strictly dictates the opinions and decisions of the appellate courts, or lower courts for that matter. Law does dictate court decisions...when and where convenient.   A one word (AFFIRMED), non-appealable decision appears to be the lazy judge's way out. The appellate judges don't really have to read in depth or closely scrutinize the appeal if a written opinion isn't forthcoming. These judges say they have too large a case load. If the courts have too large a case load, then hire more legal clerks and expand the number of judges on the appellate level. Lets have written opinions on every case. I question whether the appellate judges really read the majority of appeals or just have their law clerks peruse them and suggest which ones should require written opinions. Incidentally, I've had several lower court judges agree with my above stated rationalization of the appellate courts.

Everything being equal, the same appellate brief, etc., the only difference being that one case is being represented by an attorney and the other by a Pro Se Litigant, the odds for winning an appeal are greatly enhanced with the signature of the attorney on the documents. The legal fraternity will vehemently deny this statement.

I must admit that the level of strict law and procedure are enhanced a notch or two when one goes the appellate route in the judicial system.   It is nearly imperative that you at least have the guidance of a competent paralegal when undertaking this endeavor as a Pro Se Litigant. The Rules of Appellate Procedure are the guidelines for this adventure.   The State Rules of Civil Procedure are still appropriate but where there may be conflict, the Rules of Civil Procedure are subordinate to the Rules of Appellate Procedure in the appellate courts.   I will not belabor the appellate process other than generalities in this primer.   An appeal is a discipline within itself, an exacting science. If your desire is to go through an appeal by yourself, I would strongly urge you at the extreme least to take an academic course or read and understand a book on the basics in *Legal Writing and Research*.   You should read, know and understand the Rules of Appellate Procedure in your appellate jurisdiction.   Even having followed this advice, you are going to have a rough row to hoe. Otherwise, I would hire a competent independent paralegal or attorney to write the appellate brief (appeal). Be prepared to pay a healthy sum for this service. Depending on the subject matter, we're talking about a contribution of significant man hours of legal research and writing.

If a lawyer has an emotional client whom he can convince got screwed in the ruling by the local judge, the lawyer will bring to the attention of the client that the appeals court might probably reverse the lower court decision. In such an emotional state, the client's concern for the financial cost of an appeal tends to be secondary in importance. Sure, the attorney would like to say he won on appeal but what the hell, he's going to be financially enhanced win or lose! Following a losing decision from the appellate court and after picking up his remaining balance of legal fees, the attorney will usually tell the client some bullshit story like, "We gave it our best shot but the deck was stacked against us." or "We prevailed on law and substance but they just didn't understand our basis of law."

Always get a second opinion before launching into the appellate process. There are numerous stories about clients having to continue paying legal fees from an appellate process venture long after the decision was handed down by the courts.

An integral part of the appellate process is the *record.* The record refers to the evidence presented at trial in the lower court or the court whose decision you are appealing. This includes the verbiage said during the trial which is taken down verbatim by a court reporter. It is up to you to have hired the court reporter for this purpose unless the other side has already done this. The initial cost of having a court reporter at trial is usually not very much. The greater cost comes if and when you decide to appeal the judge's ruling and, therefore, must have the court reporter's notes transcribed. If you appeal without a record of the trail, you have a 99% chance of the appellate court not even accepting your action for appeal let alone reversing the lower court decision. And remember, you can not add any more evidence to the record on appeal than was put in the record during trial.

Let me share with you an incident which recently took place regarding the appellate process. An acquaintance of mine hired an attorney to represent her in divorce proceedings against her husband. She kept me apprised of the entire scenario, trial, etc. There were no minor children involved and limited assets. The husband owned several real properties and two vehicles. She was positive that he had a financial account in a Swiss bank but could not prove it. The judge ruled that she should get half of the marital assets which included one vehicle and a condominium. In actuality she was getting about 30% of the net marital assets but she was happy with that. It was obvious to me that her female attorney was incompetent. This was apparent from a myriad of factors that occurred during the discovery process and subsequently during the trial phase. The trial concluded and the judge ordered the husband's attorney to write the final judgment. I advised the wife to make sure that her attorney confirmed that the final judgment had findings of fact supporting the division of the assets to preclude any future problems should the husband file an appeal. She passed this advice on to her attorney who did not act accordingly. You should have seen the final judgment that the judge executed. No findings of fact whatsoever.

Prior to the judge rendering the final judgment the husband had intimated that he would file an appeal if the judge signed the final judgment as orally presented. Based on just this threat, the wife's attorney hired an appellate lawyer for advice "just in case an appeal was filed by the husband". The wife's attorney did not get the wife's approval to do this, she just went ahead and hired this appellate lawyer on her own for the fee of $600. The wife asked me about this and I advised her to tell her lawyer where she could stick that $600 bill. While all of this was happening, the husband filed a notice of appeal on his own with no attorney based on no "findings of fact" being in the final judgment. The wife's attorney told her not to worry as the appellate lawyer would handle this appeal process for the wife for $10,000. The wife came to me for advice. I told her that she should do nothing right now and wait to see what the husband does. He has 60 days from the notice of appeal to file his brief. He must get the court reporter to transcribe the record and have the Clerk of the Circuit Court send it up to the district court of appeals with the file. Even after he files his brief, which I doubted he would, the wife didn't even need to look at it. It will definitely be a PCA (per curium affirmed) ruling which means the lower court decision stands. With no transcript record the wife doesn't need to waste her time nor money on an answer to the husband's brief. Well, the husband filed a brief which he authored by himself (and it looked like it) without the transcript. The wife did nothing, no answer, no hiring of an appeals attorney...nothing. And guess what? The district court of appeals returned its decision as PCA and the lower court final judgment was affirmed.

The wife saved $10,000 and an additional $600 by not needlessly hiring the appellate attorney as advised by her lawyer. When the wife told her attorney that she would not need an appellate attorney if her husband did not file the transcript with the appellate court, her attorney told her that the district court of appeals did not really need the transcript to rule in the husband's favor. The wife's attorney advised immediate hiring of the recommended appellate attorney. It makes you wonder if in fact the wife's attorney had the standard 20% ($2,000) referral fee on the line. The wife works at a retail clothing store making less that $300 a week and this scumbag attorney is trying to drain her for all she can. Incidentally, during the attorney fees hearing which I forced the wife to demand from her attorney, the judge inferred that the high legal fees charged by her attorney for such a limited and simple marital case was highly suspect and questionable. Nevertheless, the judge let the fees stand. The judicial system will do anything to help cover sucking moneys out of society into the legal fraternity coffers.

Let me share with you a few decisions of the appellate courts that are of interest. There are literally thousands of such appellate rulings in these United States but time and space preclude me from exposing them at this time.

It has been about 260 years since anyone in the U.S. was put in prison for debt (Debtor's Prison). However, incarceration can be ordered by the courts for non-payment of alimony and/or child support if one has the "ability to pay". The 4th District Court of Appeal in Florida made an interesting ruling on Aug. 2, 2000 regarding lawyer's fees in a divorce. Even though Article I, Section 11 of the Florida Constitution specifically prohibits imprisonment for debt, this Court ruled differently. The Court rationalized in its cite ...[A]llowing contempt for enforcement of an order awarding attorney's fees (and imprisonment) because the duty to pay arose out of a personal duty owed to both the former spouse or child and to society rather than a debt within a meaning of Article I, Section 11 of the Florida

Constitution.[69] Give me a break. Do the Courts cover the lawyers' ass when it comes to money or what? What a great country this is for lawyers! And in confirmation and acknowledgment of these continuing acts by the courts, the Florida 2nd District Court of Appeal[70] stated, "We are deeply troubled that circuit courts continue to *illegally* incarcerate people for civil contempt in the face not only of ample case law, but also a rule which clearly delineates the procedures that should be followed in order to ensure that the due process rights of alleged contemnors are protected." The 2nd District Court of Appeal should also be troubled with the fact that appellate courts affirm these actions.

Even though it's your constitutional right to represent yourself in a court of law in this country do you really believe the courts will honor this right? Recently an individual representing himself on the appellate level pursuant to a way of necessity (easement to his house) was denied by the Florida 5th District Court of Appeals with this sage comment on December 1, 2000: "Mr. Chodos chose to appear *pro se* in a matter that requires a complete understanding of a statutory provision which justly imposes an extraordinary burden on one seeking access by a statutory way of necessity. Regretfully, he did not seek the assistance of competent legal counsel to satisfy those requirements." In other words, put money in some attorney's pocket to represent you, dude, and we'll probably rule your way.[71] Incidentally, how do you like the appellate court inserting the word competent in front of legal counsel in their opinion. Does this infer that there are incompetent attorneys amongst us?

It is unbelievable the number of appeals that are filed by attorneys with no accompanying record. The district court automatically affirms the lower court decision in these cases. The attorney knows this but the client does not. Bottomline is that the

---

[69] Wertkin v. Wertkin, Vol. 25, No. 32, D1809, Fla. 4th DCA 2000

[70] Bresch v. Henderson, Fla. Law Wkly D1342 June 2, 2000

[71] Chodos v. Kjenslie, Fla. Law Wkly D2766, 5th DCA Florida 2000

pockets of the lawyer are lined at the expense of the unknowing client. To confirm this action, just go to your local Law Weekly, cites of recent appellate decision. There you will note a number of PCA decisions due to lack of a record (transcript).

BANKRUPTCY

Bankruptcy, in essence, means you can't pay your bills with what resources you've got. There are several forms of bankruptcy, such as Chapter 7, Chapter 11, and Chapter 13. The most common form and the one which I will discuss here is Chapter 7, personal bankruptcy. You must remember that bankruptcy is a federal action and not a state or local action. Federal laws govern it's procedure but certain of the federal laws often refer to state law. An example is the choice a debtor (person declaring bankruptcy) has in choosing certain exemptions he is allowed when filing for bankruptcy. He can choose either the exemptions allowed by federal law or the exemptions allowed for this action under state law. Some states are very liberal in their exemptions and tend to be havens for those declaring personal bankruptcy. Florida is an example of such a state. Your local law library can discern the state exemptions allowed verses the federal exemptions allowed. You can not have both and must decide which you prefer and are most advantageous to you.

Folks who move to Florida with the intent of declaring personal bankruptcy will sometimes purchase an expensive home before hand. The State of Florida bankruptcy exemptions permit the debtor to keep their homestead (residence) regardless of its value. The homestead property on which the house structure is located is limited in size depending on whether it is located within a municipality or in an unincorporated area. Typically the land size allowable within a municipality is one quarter acre while outside this jurisdiction it is 160 acres.

Even though bankruptcy legal kits are sold in office supply stores, I know of a rare few who have successfully handled their own Chapter 7, personal bankruptcy from start to finish with no help from an independent paralegal or attorney. The bankruptcy courts wallow in the good ole boy syndrome. The bankruptcy courts appear to compete with the divorce courts in financially lining the pockets of the legal fraternity. First of all, they have tried to make the bankruptcy process as procedurally complicated as possible when, in fact, it is a relatively simple process. Secondly, too much discretion is left up to the trustee and the bankruptcy judge.

We handled Chapter 7, personal bankruptcy for a number of years but ceased October 1994 when the new amended bankruptcy laws were passed by the U. S. Congress. Our fees for a simple Chapter 7 bankruptcy were $150 for either a single person or married couple. We had the typical computer software bankruptcy program. Average amount of time to take all of the information from the debtor, put it into the computer and have the package ready to file was about an hour and a half. Attorneys in our area charge between $650 and $1,500 or whatever they feel the traffic will bear for the same, identical package. Of course, the attorney will accompany you to court and hold your hand for the 30 second appearance before the trustee and/or bankruptcy judge. If you are literate enough to be able to sign your own name or read an English newspaper, you really don't need a high priced lawyer holding your hand in the bankruptcy court. Incidentally, we still do Chapter 7 personal bankruptcy packages for attorneys for $75. They send us their bankruptcy clients' data and information and we plug it into the computer. The attorneys take these completed packages and charge their clients $650 on up to whatever they think they can get away with. With the attorney's name on the documents, the bankruptcy slides through the bankruptcy procedure post haste with no problem. The same documents without the attorney's name on them, just the Pro Se Litigant's name, are closely scrutinized and often are rejected by the trustee and/or bankruptcy judge before it's all over.

Why did we stop doing personal bankruptcies for Pro Se Litigants? Because the newly amended bankruptcy law stated that the bankruptcy judge at his discretion could fine up to $1,000 and incarcerate any non-lawyer that aided anyone in a bankruptcy proceeding. The bankruptcy lawyers nationwide were losing enormous sums of money in that "Joe Six-pack" started going to independent paralegals for their Chapter 7 bankruptcies. Why not? $150 sure beats hell out of $1,000 for the same end result. The local state Bar could not go after these independent paralegals for the unlicensed (unauthorized) practice of law (UPL) because bankruptcy is a federal action and not a state action. The only way to curb these funds from flowing away from the legal fraternity was to have the Congress (mostly lawyers themselves) pass a stringent federal law. And Congress obliged. They didn't say non-lawyers could not do bankruptcies for folks. In essence, the new law said the bankruptcy judge at his whim and discretion could fine a non-lawyer up to a $1,000 and incarcerate him for up to a year in jail if the judge did not like the way an "i" was dotted or "t" crossed. The new law was very effective and accomplished the bankruptcy attorney's purpose. Nearly all independent paralegals ceased providing this personal bankruptcy service to Pro Se Litigants. Judicial interpretation of the new bankruptcy law gave the attorneys an avenue to file actions against non-lawyers (independent paralegals) who continued to prepare bankruptcy documents for Pro Se Litigants. Even if the independent paralegal's bankruptcy paper work is impeccably correct, the attorney can file an action with the bankruptcy court against the independent paralegal for the most mundane, inconsequential reason. The judge will more than likely award the attorney $1,000 to be paid by the non-lawyer. The attorney can even group such actions together for one hearing and be awarded a cumulative sum of money or fines taken from the non-lawyers. Senior Florida Bankruptcy Judge Alexander L. Paskay of the Middle District Bankruptcy Court of Florida is on record saying the following at a bankruptcy continuing legal education seminar luncheon for lawyers in Tampa, Florida on January 20, 1995, several months after passage of the new bankruptcy law. "[N]ow is designed draconian measures against preparers (independent paralegals/non-lawyers). Kind that's also good for the lawyer because you are now awarded a bounty or a bonus of $1,000 if you are to go after preparers and obtain and establishing that they violated the very stringent requirements which will not be very difficult to prove in my judgment. The law permits an award of damages to the debtor $2,000 per violation or twice the amount they charge which is probably $800 or $900 plus $1,000 attorney fee for attorney who is doing it. So all you have to do is file ten of them, file a motion to consolidate, you get ten thousand bucks to try one in half hour which ain't chicken feed, if you ask me. Pretty good deal. Here are a little practice hints. They are free." and "[I]f product of this Commission (Bankruptcy Commission) is gonna be just as fuzzy and bad as the last one, then it would be a relief bill for attorneys because it has so many provisions that's wide open to subject and debate and hopefully for you all, fruitful and paying litigation...." and "...need translator (for 1994 Bankruptcy Amendment)." and "[T]here are bothersome aspects I mentioned about Amendment 523(a) under discharge divorce business...." This is a federal bankruptcy judge making these disparaging remarks. Hard to believe, isn't it? I've had clients wanting me to handle their bankruptcy documents tell me that the reason they are declaring bankruptcy is because they are broke and can't come up with the $1,000 for the attorney in addition to the $160 filing fee. Then again, I've heard a bankruptcy attorney say, "I really don't give a damn whether or not some broke bastard can or can not afford to pay my fee for bankruptcy."

The bankruptcy judge is the person who makes the final decisions in bankruptcy cases, excepting of course unless you want to file an appeal with the next higher court (federal District Court of Appeals). For our purposes here, forget an appeal. In an appeal you're really talking about big bucks and paying for lawyers' airplanes and Jaguars. The bankruptcy judge is not elected, he is appointed. It is one of many political plums available in the federal political environment. And even as a layman, if you attend some bankruptcy hearings in your area and watch the judge operate, you will note that competency is not a primary criterion to getting this appointment.

The Trustee in a personal bankruptcy is usually an attorney who is the focal point of your bankruptcy process. This is another non-elected position awarded via the political appointment process. Again, competency is not a requirement to appointment as a trustee. The trustee's discretion in determining the facts in your case is scary. The trustee is the bankruptcy court official with which you will deal directly.

Their demeanor varies from jurisdiction to jurisdiction. There is a trustee in the Middle District of Florida that is a genuine, certified, discriminatory incompetent. If you have an attorney representing you, it's a slam dunk and you virtually will have no problems. If you are representing yourself as a Pro Se Litigant, lookout! You wouldn't believe the harassment to which you will be subjected by this trustee.

The Chapter 7, personal bankruptcy process should be relatively simple. After the proper documents have been filled out and you have executed them, you file them at your main federal district bankruptcy office with the Bankruptcy Clerk. In our district the filing fee is $160. If you are indigent and can't afford to pay the filing fee, the Bankruptcy Clerk can handle that. If you can't pay the entire fee at one time, they usually have a payment plan for that, also. Shortly after filing, your creditors (folks you owe) will be notified via mail by the bankruptcy court that you have filed for personal bankruptcy, what your intentions are and the date of the creditors hearing. By intentions, I mean whether you are requesting to write off (not pay) the creditors debt or possibly reaffirm the debt. Reaffirm means you do not want to write off the debt; you want to pay it off. An example is the mortgage on your home or vehicle. The debtor and creditor should execute a reaffirm document. In the example above, your home and vehicle are considered secured debts which you may retain if you keep making the monthly payments as originally contracted with the creditor. A secured debt is one in which you owe money on something tangible like real property or an automobile. An unsecured debt is generally a credit card debt, an unsecured personal loan or a hospital bill.

You will be notified via mail of the date of the creditors hearing which usually takes place in less than 3 months after your initial filing. A creditor usually has 60 days after notification of the creditor hearing to file a claim against the estate (assets) of the debtor. A creditor has a limited amount of time in which to file an objection to the final Discharge of Bankruptcy before he is shut out. Unless there are mitigating circumstances and your case is unusual, the only creditor that I've experienced who always makes an appearance at the creditor hearing is Sears. Apparently, Sears keeps an employee at all of these personal bankruptcy hearings. The trustee is the top dog at the creditors hearing and rules with an iron hand. Now you must remember from whence the trustee comes. The trustee has a vested interest in these creditor hearings. The trustee personally pockets an estimated $45 on every personal bankruptcy case that comes before him. If your case is like the majority of the cases where the debtor doesn't have a pot to pee in or a window in which to throw it out, you won't be in front of the trustee 30 seconds. The trustee might ask you your name and some other stupid question and then say "Next". If any of your creditors make an appearance at this meeting, they have the right to question you. Incidentally, all conversations in front of the trustee are taped recorded; don't get caught in a lie. If you encounter no problems at the creditor meeting, you will either be notified of a hearing in front of the bankruptcy judge for some more bureaucratic mumbo jumbo or you will be mailed a final Discharge of Bankruptcy. If you have any problems with creditors, you will probably have to appear before the judge. If you do have any potentially significant problems with a creditor, it might behoove you to contact an independent paralegal or competent bankruptcy attorney for advice before your appearance in front of the judge and/or trustee. In your jurisdiction it may just be normal procedure to have to appear in front of the bankruptcy judge for your final discharge of bankruptcy. Then it's all over and you can start your life over again.

There are many caveats in declaring personal bankruptcy. First of all, the trustee tends to be greedy. For example, the law lets you keep up to a $1,000 equity in your vehicle. In other words, if your are driving around town in your fully paid for $120,000 Ferrari, they gonna get that vehicle, boy. But if your clunker is a 1982 model worth about $900, the trustee must let you keep it for your transportation to and from work. Let's say your vehicle is worth an estimated $1,200 and that is what you state in your bankruptcy documents. Most trustees will overlook the excess $200 allowed but I have seen trustees that were genuinely greedy and would legally demand you put $200 in excess of the $1,000 into the court coffers to compensate for going over the stipulated $1,000 allowable limit. You've got to understand that the trustee personally gets to pocket 10% of your assets that he gets put into the bankruptcy coffer. These funds, less the amount skimmed off by the trustee, are usually given to the creditors on a pro rata basis to cover some of your debts. This example holds true to all of your exemptions. If the trustee can sell a piece of your property for $500,000, the trustee gets to keep $50,000 for himself and his personal use. I mean it's ALL his. He doesn't have to share the $50,000 with the court or anyone else. The previously mentioned $200 excess doesn't sound like much when the trustee only gets to keep 10% of it but it's like Senator Everett Dirksen used to say in referring to government spending, "A billion dollars here and a billion dollars there, and before you know it, it adds up to real money!" The trustee also has the right to send someone to your residence to take an accounting of all of your household furnishing and personal property. They don't usually exercise this right unless your declared household furnishings tend to significantly surpass the permitted exempted value. Needless to say, if you have a $50,000 stamp collection at home which they find and you didn't declare it, you've got a problem.

As in any other aspect of the legal process, those affiliated with the legal system usually tend to give Pro Se Litigants a hard time. The bankruptcy court is no different. This is especially true of the typical trustee. Have you ever seen the nerd who was beat up by everyone in the neighborhood when they were a kid? They were powerless and could never stand up for themselves. Then they become adults and end up with some authoritative position such as trustee or judge in the bankruptcy court. Is it any wonder a good many of these officials want to throw their weight around in a room full of poor, bankrupt Pro Se Litigants that are emotionally distraught, intimidated, and damn sure don't know what the hell is going on?

Sometimes a creditor or their attorney will keep harassing you with phone calls, letters or even a law suit about your debt to them after they have been sent a notice informing them of your pending bankruptcy. This is a no-no with potential severe federal penalties. Once you file for bankruptcy there is imposed on your estate by the court what is called an automatic stay. No creditor is supposed to contact you relative to your debt without the court's permission, such as approval of a motion to lift the automatic stay. If you do hear from a creditor after filing for bankruptcy, I would immediately send them a

Suggestion of Bankruptcy and file a copy of same with the bankruptcy court. Following is a copy of a Suggestion of Bankruptcy to a creditor who filed a law suit against a debtor after he filed for bankruptcy.

IN THE CIRCUIT COURT OF THE THIRTIETH JUDICIAL CIRCUIT, IN AND FOR SLOP COUNTY, FLORIDA

RAPE BANK,
            Plaintiff,

                                                Case No. 92-5439-CA

vs.

JOHN DOE,
            Defendant,

SUGGESTION OF BANKRUPTCY

Debtor, JOHN DOE, hereby files his Suggestion of Bankruptcy and states as follows:

1.   Debtor filed for protection under the United States Bankruptcy Code which case is styled as follows:

UNITED STATES BANKRUPTCY COURT
MIDDLE DISTRICT OF FLORIDA, CLERMONT DIVISION

IN RE:

JOHN DOE,   CASE NO. 0622657070-06-94
_____/Debtor
2. This action is subject to the automatic stay of 11 U.S. C. Section 362.

CERTIFICATE OF SERVICE

I HEREBY CERTIFY that a true and correct copy of the foregoing has been furnished to RAPE BANK at 123 E. Jess St., Clermont, Florida 34444 by U. S. Mail Regular Delivery, mailed this nth day of July, 19yy.

_____
JOHN DOE, Pro Se Litigant
address

Occasionally a creditor or his agent will continue to harass you after you have been granted your Discharge of Bankruptcy. If they continue this action after you have mailed them a copy of your Discharge of Bankruptcy, you can either send them a letter similar to the following letter or hire an attorney to sue them.

CERTIFIED MAIL NO. 12344556778
RECEIPT REQUESTED

February nth, 19xx

Greedy Pockets, Esquire
Attorney at Law
Post Office Box 24567890
Anytown, Georgia 343434

Re: John Doe, Acct. #8765432.
Dear Mr. Pockets:
Mr. Pro Se Litigant filed for protection under Chapter 7 (personal bankruptcy), Title 11, United States Bankruptcy Code on or about April yth, 19yy. On August zth, 19yy, Mr. Litigant was discharged

of his scheduled debts by Honor Me, Bankruptcy Judge of the United States Bankruptcy Court, Middle District of Florida, Clermont Division (copy enclosed). The discharged scheduled debts included CENTRAL PRODUCTS, INC.

Central Products, Inc. and/or any of its lawful agents failed upon notification by the United States Bankruptcy Court to seek relief from the automatic stay pursuant to 11 U.S.C. Section 362(d). Nor did the creditor file a complaint objecting to discharge within the appropriate time element pursuant to 11 U.S.C. Section 727. Mr. Pro Se Litigant hereby alleges he is being damaged by "willful violation" of Title 11, United States Bankruptcy Code. *The penalties for violating Title 11, United States Bankruptcy Code can extend to punitive damages, and these may be applied as against attorneys as well as the creditor or its respective agents.*

BE ADVISED, if Central Products, Inc. and any of its lawful agents do not remove Mr. Pro Se Litigant from their credit list (report #75858585) as being delinquent as above stated within 5 days after receipt of this demand notice, Mr. Pro Se Litigant will have no alternative but to seek legal recourse in the Middle District Federal Court of Florida. You along with Central Products, Inc., Getem Credit Corporation et al will be enjoined from further activity in this matter and Mr. Pro Se Litigant will pray the court for damages, both actual and punitive, in addition to but not limited to costs and attorney fees.

Sincerely,

BIG BOB

Immediate positive results were forthcoming within 3 days after receipt of the above letter by the attorney representing the creditor! One did not have to be a rocket scientist to understand the content of the letter and its potential ramifications.

As a point of information at this time I would like to include information to help you if you happen to get caught up in a similar scenario as this. Even though the Discharge of Bankruptcy might absolve you from various debts, it is up to you to motion the bankruptcy court for specific removal of liens. Following are examples of the required documents to effect removal of a lien from your residence which was recorded prior to your bankruptcy and subsequently discharged by the bankruptcy court.

Pro Se Litigant
333 Sixth Street
Clermont, Florida 33334

UNITED STATES BANKRUPTCY COURT
MIDDLE DISTRICT OF THE STATE OF FLORIDA

In Re:	)	Case No.
99-54993-617		
PRO SE LITIGANT,	)	Chapter 7
Debtor,	)	
	)	
_____	)	
GETTEM, BLEEDEM & HOWE, P.A.	)	Adv. Pro.
No. _____		
Plaintiff,	)	
	)	
vs.	)	
	)	
PRO SE LITIGANT,	)	
Defendant.	)	
_____	)	

MOTION TO AVOID JUDICIAL LIEN

1. Debtor, PRO SE LITIGANT, commenced this case on September 7, 1992 by filling a voluntary petition for relief under Chapter 7 of Title 11 of the United States Code.

2. This Court has jurisdiction over this notion, filed pursuant to 11 U.S.C. Section 522(f) to avoid and cancel a judicial lien held by GETTEM, BLEEDEM & HOWE , P.A., on real property used as the debtor's residence, under 28 U.S.C. Section 1334.

3. On April 16, 1991, creditors recorded a judicial lien against debtor's residence at 333 Sixth Street, Clermont, Florida 33334. The said judicial lien is entered of record as follows:

Wannaby County Court of the Thirtieth Circuit Court in and for Wannaby County, Florida, Case No. CO 90-2993, lien amount of $11,802.89, recorded April 16, 1991.

4. The debtor's interest in the property referred to in the preceding paragraph and encumbered by the lien has been claimed as fully exempt in their bankruptcy case.

5. The existence of GETTEM, BLEEDEM & HOWE, P.A.'s lien on debtor's real property impairs exemptions to which the debtor would be entitled under 11 U.S.C. Section 522(b).

WHEREFORE, debtor prays for an order against GETTEM, BLEEDEM & HOWE, P.A. avoiding and canceling the judicial lien in the above-mentioned property, and for such additional or alternative relief as may be just and proper.

Dated:_____

_____
PRO SE LITIGANT, Debtor/Defendant

Similar to state courts, due process must be observed here. Therefore, the bankruptcy court requires proof of service.

Of course, with any motion submitted to the courts, a good Pro Se Litigant submits an order and notice of hearing as follows (captions not included):

ORDER AVOIDING JUDICIAL LIEN

The motion of the above named debtor, PRO SE LITIGANT, to avoid the lien of the respondent, GETTEM, BLEEDEM & HOWE, P.A., is sustained.

IT IS HEREBY ORDERED AND DECREED that the judicial lien held by Gettem, Bleedem & Howe, P.A., in and on debtor's residential real estate at 333 Sixth Street, Clermont, Florida 33334, entered of record at the Wannaby County Court of the Thirtieth Circuit Court in and for Wannaby County, Florida at Clermont, Florida on April 16, 1991, Case No. 90-2993 for the sum of $11,802.89 be hereby canceled.

It is further ORDERED that unless debtor's bankruptcy case is dismissed, Gettem, Bleedem & Howe, P.A. shall take all steps necessary and appropriate to release the judicial lien and remove it from the local judgment index.

Dated:_____

_____
U. S. Bankruptcy Judge

Next comes the notice of hearing(caption not included):

Legal Whores

NOTICE OF MOTION TO AVOID JUDICIAL LIEN

TO: Gettem, Bleedem & Howe, P.A.
199976 S. Greed Ave.
Dollars, Florida 038899

PLEASE TAKE NOTICE that the undersigned will bring a motion to avoid judicial lien for hearing before this Court in Room _____, United States Courthouse located at 532 W. South Ave., Clermont, Florida 33454 on _____, 1992 at _____A./P.M., or as soon thereafter as debtor can be heard.

Dated:_____

_____
PRO SE LITIGANT, Debtor

As the Certificate of Service statement is used in state courts affirming deliverance of certain judicial documents to various parties, the Proof Of Service By Mail is similar in nature in the federal bankruptcy court. However, in the bankruptcy court scene the person affirming the deliverance of the document must be over the age of eighteen years and a disinterested party to the case at hand. Following is a copy of Proof Of Service By Mail (caption not included):

PROOF OF SERVICE BY MAIL
I, Sally Mae, declare that: I am a resident in the County of Wannaby, State of Florida. My residence address is 999 Chicka Trail, Mongoose, Florida 35678. I am over the age of eighteen years and I am not a party to this case.

On October 3, 1992, I served the Notice Of Motion and Motion To Avoid Judicial Lien on Gettem, Bleedem & Howe, P.A., by placing true and correct copies thereof enclosed in a sealed envelope with postage thereon fully prepaid, in the United States Mail at Clermont, Florida Post Office, addressed as follows:

Gettem, Bleedem & Howe, P.A.
199976 S. Greed Ave.
Dollars, Florida 038899

I declare under penalty of perjury that the foregoing is true and correct, and that this declaration was executed on the _____ day of _____, 1992, at Clermont, Wannaby County, Florida.

_____
SALLY MAE

Books have been written about bankruptcy and are available for reference in your public law library. The above is just a very basic primer on personal bankruptcy which I trust will give the reader a quick brush with the aspects of this action.

Legal Whores

LANDLORD/TENANT EVICTIONS

Seems like everyone is after the no good, money grubbin' property owner or landlord. While some of them do need a good ass kicking as slum landlords, the vast majority are hard working folks who are not on welfare, drugs, or after freebies from the market place or government. Usually they have worked, sacrificed, saved and took risk to own the rental property they have. They need the income (rents) from their respective properties to pay the rental properties' monthly bills such as mortgage, taxes, insurance, repairs and who knows what other costs that tend to inevitably and unexpectedly pop up. Just remember, if there are no landlords, then there are no tenants because there are no rentals available. It's just like I tell people when they start bad mouthing those terrible corporations, "If there aren't any employers, then there damn sure aren't going to be any employees." Think about it.

At this juncture in this chapter I would like to interject a "letter to the editor" from the Florida Bar News[72]. I consider it enlightening insofar as how lawyers sometimes fit into this eviction picture. The letter is from attorney Mark Warda. "All of us who have represented landlords know how pro bono and legal aid lawyers can waste the courts' time and landlords' money with meritless claims, the only purpose of which is to help the delinquent tenant live a few more months at the landlord's expense. The goal is not in any way justice, it is rape of responsible members of society by the irresponsible, legally sanctioned and promoted by the Florida Bar. Many landlords are not rich, but

---

[72] 4/15/97

135

merely struggling entrepreneurs who have managed to save a small down payment and fixed up a dilapidated house for their future. While the tenant lives for free they pay the mortgage, insurance, taxes and water out of their paychecks.

Rather than improve the image of lawyers such cases put the entire legal system in question and give those who are granted free legal services the mistaken belief that they are owed something by the rest of society. I suggest that lawyers' time would be better spent teaching them courses on budgeting, prioritizing, and personal responsibility." Excellent comment from a lawyer!

I will not discuss commercial evictions here because there is usually a lot of leeway in the legal process to evict a commercial tenant. In many cases commercial evictions follow the same procedures as with residential evictions. Be forewarned, however, if the tenant is evicted and leaves personal property at the leased premises, replevin might be needed. Replevin is a legal process whereby you can legally take, move, sell, etc. the vacated tenant's personal property from the leased premises. *DO NOT* remove this personal property from the premises unless you know exactly what you are doing and the subsequent potential legal ramifications. If not sure, phone your attorney.

The Florida Supreme Court has ruled that a property manager authorized by the property owner can file with the courts actions for eviction from residential premises for non-payment of rent if the action is not contested by the tenant. This means under these given circumstances you don't require a lawyer. We charge $145 for such a residential eviction and can usually have the tenant off the leased premises within 15 days. Lawyers usually charge $400 - $600 and take on average 45 - 60 days. We initiate these cases immediately and follow it through the court process on a daily basis. The attorney can not afford to give the everyday residential eviction the special attention we do.

In Florida, the Rules of Civil Procedure (and Florida Statutes, of course) still prevail in residential evictions. However, every little jurisdiction (county court) has its own nuances and local administrative guidelines for evictions and small claims. You could probably appeal these local nuances to the higher courts and win but just go ahead and do it like the local judges and Clerk of the Court want it done. In our locale, residential eviction documents include Summons, 5 Day Complaint, 20 Day Complaint, Service of Process, 3 Day notice, Lease, Non-Military Affidavit, Affidavit of Indebtedness, Writ of Possession, Final Judgment for Possession, Final Judgment, Default, Certificate of Mailing, Certificate of Indebtedness, several stamped, self-addressed envelopes for the tenant and you, and authorization from the property owner if you are a property manager. To me it would be a lot easier and quicker to shoot the son-of-a-bitch for not paying the rent rather than trying to evict him. But then how would the judges be able to flex their court room power or lawyers extend their financial prowess in the eviction arena?

The summons and service of process are common to most causes and actions and have been discussed previously. The 5 Day Complaint means you are alleging the tenant has not paid his rent on time and you want possession of the premises. The tenant has 5 days from being served the complaint to file his answer with the court and pay into the registry of the court (Clerk's office) the amount of rent in dispute. If the tenant fails to do this, and most do, then you file a motion for default, Final Judgment for Possession (type INSTANTER on the judgment somewhere in order to expedite it) and a Writ of Possession. Usually the judge will sign the Final Judgment for Possession in a couple of days at which time the Clerk will issue the Writ of Possession to the local Sheriff. We have to pay the Sheriff $70 to serve the Writ of Possession on the tenant in this area. You will get copies in the mail from the Sheriff affirming the dates of service of the complaint and Writ of Possession. Don't hesitate to phone the Sheriff's office to find out exactly when service has been made. Here in Florida, the tenant has 24 hours from the time the Writ of Possession has been served to remove himself and his belongings off the rented premises. If he is still there, the landlord or authorized agent has the legal right to physically remove the tenant and his personal effects off the premises (into the road right-of-way). If it comes to this, I would strongly advise having a Deputy Sheriff present in case of any potential altercation. Better yet, hire a couple of 300 pound local high school football players to help in the move. If the judge refuses to sign the Final Judgment of

Possession or the Clerk refuses to issue the Writ of Possession under the above given conditions, you have several alternatives. You can appeal to the next higher court, you can file a Motion for Clarification wanting to know what the hell the problem is, you can pull out your check book and hire an attorney, or you just forget about the whole thing and let the dude live there rent free. If the judge is at fault or jerking your chain because you are representing yourself, I would absolutely, definitely file a complaint with the State Supreme Court or whatever judicial or political body that hear such complaints. Usually this body won't really do anything, but the paper work for the judge is a real pain and the news media might pick it up.

Let's say your tenant has moved out during this eviction process. In your original filing you should have filed the summons, 5 Day Complaint, 20 Day Complaint, Service of Process, Non-Military Affidavit, Lease, 3 Day Notice, envelopes, and Certificate of Mailing. Five days after service on the tenant and no answer from him, you file a motion for default, Final Judgment for Possession and Writ of Possession. Twenty days after he was served with the eviction complaints, and he has not answered the 20 day complaint, which is usually the case, you file with the Clerk a motion for default, Affidavit of Indebtedness, and Final Judgment. The 20 day complaint is for breach of contract (the lease) and you want damages which is usually back rent. It is incumbent on you to put in the amount of indebtedness in the Affidavit of Indebtedness and the Final Judgment. There should be blanks for principal, interest, attorney fees, court costs, and damages. Be careful about what you put in these blanks because the judges are just looking for ways to dismiss your complaint and tell you to go hire an attorney. Here is an example.

This Landlord hired us to complete the paper work for eviction of a residential tenant. Everything went smoothly and according to plan right down to the judge signing the Final Judgment for back rent. The judge returned the unsigned, properly filled out final judgment to the landlord with the comment, "No interest amount is shown in the Final Judgment and this must be corrected". I had the landlord phone the judge's secretary to see if perhaps there was some mistake. It was our understanding that under the given circumstances, the landlord did not have to charge interest on back rent if he didn't want to. The judge's legal assistant said, "Make the judge happy and put something down". We put in the final judgment "that shall bear interest at the rate of 8% per year" and returned it to the judge. Subsequently, the judge returned this final judgment back to the landlord with the comment "This is not acceptable". On convincing the landlord that this judge was just trying to play games with a Pro Se Litigant, we filed a Motion for Clarification which I must share with you (caption deleted):

MOTION FOR CLARIFICATION

COMES NOW the plaintiff, JOHN DOE, and requests clarification of this Court's refusal to accept and execute a Final Judgment for Plaintiff and would say:

1. That on or about April nth, 19xx, Plaintiff filed in this jurisdiction an Eviction Summons/Residential (5 day) and Eviction of Tenant For Non-payment of Rent (20 day) along with other required documents.

2. That there was no timely answer form the Defendants in this action, therefore, a Motion for Default was filed with the Clerk of the Court and A Default was entered on both Count I (5 day) and Count II (20 day). In addition to filing of the aforementioned Default, Plaintiff filed an Affidavit of Indebtedness, Non-Military Affidavit, and Final Judgment (for plaintiff).

3. That subsequent to the action taken in paragraph 2 above, this Court returned the submitted Final Judgment to the Plaintiff stating, "No interest amount is shown in the Final Judgment and this must be corrected."

4. That in an effort to comply with this Court's wishes the Plaintiff entered upon the Final Judgment "that shall bear interest at the rate of 8% per year" and returned same to this Court. Again this Court returned the Final Judgment to the Plaintiff with the inscription, "This is not acceptable."

5. That no where in Florida Statutes or case law can the Plaintiff find or locate any authority confirming that interest MUST be charged to a Defendant or by a Plaintiff in a Final Judgment for residential eviction.

WHEREFORE, the Plaintiff respectfully requests a clarification of this Court's refusal to execute the Plaintiff's Final Judgment in this action and what steps must the Plaintiff take in order to have this Court return an executed Final Judgment in favor of the Plaintiff.

_____
JOHN DOE, Plaintiff/Pro Se Litigant

We had made the determination that if this judge would not sign the final judgment now, we were going to (1) file for a rehearing, (2) file a motion for recusal (disqualification) of this county judge, (3) file a formal complaint with the Judicial Qualifications Committee, (4) file a complaint with the Chief Judge of the Circuit, and/or (5) file an appeal in the Circuit Court. Two days after receiving our Motion for Clarification, the judicial assistant phoned the landlord and asked him to please mail the final judgment to the judge for his signature. We mailed him three different types of final judgment papers with and without interest with a note saying, "Take your pick". The jerk signed one and returned the executed original to the landlord. I have had some of the Deputy Clerks at the court house tell about the lacking and inept paper work (pleadings, motions, etc.) submitted to the court house by attorneys that are accepted "as is" by the judges. But let a Pro Se Litigant misspell one word and certain judges will dismiss it. Even if the Pro Se Litigant's documents are impeccably perfect, we have found that some judges will still go to great lengths to sabotage the action.

I had another county judge in this same jurisdiction give one of my clients a hard time on a residential eviction action. The client was an authorized property manager of a certain residential property where the tenant refused to pay his rent. All the appropriate documents were filed with the court house and the tenant was served by the Sheriff. There being no timely answer from the tenant, a motion for default, Final Judgment for Possession and Writ of Possession were filed. Shortly thereafter, the judge sent a notice to the plaintiff that the case was dismissed because "The complaint was filed by a property manager but not on the Supreme Court approved forms." Here we go again with another judge who remembers when he was a lawyer and had to chase ambulances and financially milk those who didn't know any better. In other words, this was his subtle way in letting the landlord know he had better hire an attorney. I constantly see this type of discrimination against Pro Se Litigants in one form or another from the judges in the various disciplines of law. My client said "Bullshit, I'm not hiring a lawyer. What's the next modus operendi?" We filed a motion for clarification of the judge's dismissal order.

MOTION FOR CLARIFICATION OF ORDER

Plaintiff hereby respectfully requests clarification of this court's order dated the nth day of November, 20xx, pursuant to Fla. R. Civ. P. 1.540, in that

1. The order states, "The complaint is not on the Supreme Court approved forms". The Orange County Clerk of the Court has specific residential tenant eviction forms (complaint, summons, default, etc.) for non-payment of rent which are not Supreme Court approved forms. The Circuit Clerk's office will only accept the aforementioned Orange County generated residential tenant eviction forms from the Plaintiff or his property manager. Historically this court has accepted these county generated forms executed and delivered by authorized property managers in non-contested residential evictions. Does this court anticipate initiating some degree of continuity with the judges and the Clerk of the Court in this matter in the near future?

2. The order "dismissed without prejudice" subject complaint and as one reason stated "The complaint...was filed by a property manager...." Subsequent to issuance of said order, on the yth day of November, 20xx, this court's judicial assistant, Sally Dummy, informed the property manager in this action that THE FLORIDA BAR RE ADVISORY OPINION, 605 So. 2d 868 (Fla. 1992) was the cited case law by this court in determining that property managers were not authorized to complete, sign and file complaints for eviction and motion or default and to obtain final judgments and writs of possession on behalf of landlords in uncontested residential evictions for nonpayment of rent. "[P]roperty managers are hereby authorized to complete, sign and file complaints for eviction and motions for default,

and to obtain final judgments and writs of possession on behalf of landlords in uncontested residential evictions for nonpayment of rent." Id. 871. Plaintiff requests clarification of this court's order insofar as the legality of authorized property managers is concerned regarding the aforementioned actions.

_____

JACK SON, Plaintiff/Pro Se Litigant

In other words, this motion for clarification of the judge's order was saying, why don't you people get your act together, get off my case and let's conclude this action. After much "thanking" of the judge and telling him how great and wonderful a jurist he was, he signed the final judgment. What an asshole! I want the readers to understand that this type of action by the judges is very common not only in Florida but other jurisdictions as well. The examples that I am bringing to light are definitely not exceptions to the rule.

The judges fail to realize or maybe they do realize that the tenant is living rent free all this time that the judge is playing games with the Plaintiff/Pro Se Litigant. The judges' salary is not based on his competency so what the hell does he care about some Pro Se Litigant. Believe me, the vast majority don't. Incidentally, sometimes, but rarely, the landlord can be the bad guy in these evictions.

What happens in an eviction action when the tenant files an answer but does not deposit the funds (past due rent) in contention in the court as required by law during his 5 day period prior to landlord repossession? If an attorney is representing the landlord/plaintiff, the judge signs the Final Judgment for Possession and a Writ of Possession is issued immediately. The law states that the tenant must deposit said funds with the court and then a hearing will be held to ascertain who is right before proceeding with any action to evict the tenant. However, most county judges will give the tenant a hearing if the tenant writes some kind of answer even on scratch paper and files it with the court yet deposits no funds with the court as prescribed by law. The hearing date can be and is at the discretion of the judge. If a hearing is given under these conditions, the landlord needs to file a Motion to Strike immediately. This motion should quote the law and demand immediate relief. Under the given statute the tenant has no standing in court and the Final Judgment for Possession and Writ of Possession should be granted by the court to the plaintiff. Many tenants know the system and how to play the game in being able to remain on the leased premises rent free. Most of these judges need to understand what the real world is like. I put a lot of the judge's assistants and secretaries in the same category as these judges. They start thinking they are God's personal messengers instead of public servants paid with our tax dollars. Many are snotty and won't give you the time of day unless you are an attorney. They will even tell you to go hire a lawyer. I even had one hang up on me in Osceola County while I was trying to straighten out a residential eviction fau pax which the court had caused. That one was the straw that broke the camels back and affirmed my decision to write this primer. These legal beagle idiots don't want to admit that the U. S. Constitution gives you the right to represent yourself in court. However, it doesn't give you the right to waste the court's valuable time either. Always have the correct paper work and know the administrative procedures for whatever legal endeavor you initiate. Then if the legal fraternity starts jerkin' you around, stand by your guns and giv'em hell.

Depending on what the law says in your state, be careful about not returning the tenants security deposit in a residential eviction action. Florida requires that the landlord either returns to the tenant the entire security deposit or a letter defining in detail why the entire security deposit is not being returned within 15 days after the tenant has vacated the premises. Even though the tenant owes you back rent and you have a final judgment, you have to abide by the statute which refers to this scenario. It is best to do this via certified mail, return receipt requested to the last known address of the tenant. If you don't, and some shyster attorney gets to the tenant, he can initiate a legal action against you and cause you untold grief...and legal fees, both yours and the tenant's.

Just recently in a local jurisdiction in central Florida, the judiciary has started implementing a new mediation process for residential evictions. Instead of following the law as subscribed by the state legislature, the judges have decided on their own to have another step involved in this judicial process called mediation. All mediation does is prolong the process in evicting the dead beat tenants and secure additional legal fees for the attorneys. And who suffers? You got it! It's the landlord again. But then again, we have watched the judicial system on a perennial basis in the various disciplines of law, structure the modus operendi of the applicable rules of procedure in such a way as to generate more work (and fees) for the legal fraternity at the expense of efficiency and frugality for the client. Mediation my ass! It's like being a little bit pregnant: no such thing, you're either pregnant or you're not. You either owe back rent or you don't. Mediation for what...???

Here's one for the tenant that recently came into my office. This fellow, his wife and four children moved out of an apartment under the following conditions and the landlord is suing them for past due rent. The gentlemen, James, documented everything he told me in addition to having pictures for verification. The roof in the apartment was leaking profusely on his children's bed in the bedroom, a plumber was needed to stop leaks in water pipes, etc., etc. In other words the place was uninhabitable and James put the landlord on notice in writing as directed by law. The landlord refused to do anything. James moved out, 2 months before his lease was to expire. The landlord sued James for the remaining two months rent and refused to give him his security deposit. James came to me for help as the least expensive attorney wanted a $1,200 retainer. James works for the city as a laborer. He typifies a hard working, non-confrontational, nice person. His wife was about to have a nervous breakdown over this lawsuit. Firstly, I had James file a motion to dismiss because the three day notice to tenant the landlord affixed to James' door, which is statutorily required was fatally defective. It did not adhere to the requirements of the statute. Secondly, in the motion to dismiss we enumerated the actions James took as required by the law in informing the landlord of the uninhabitable condition of the apartment in writing. The law gives the landlord seven days in which to respond and begin repairs. This landlord did nothing. We filed for a hearing. At the hearing in the county court the judge was cajoling with the landlord during the hearing and would not let James tell his side of the story. Even though it was James' hearing and motion, the judge denied the motion and ordered

James to put the sued for sum into the court registry until a trial could be docketed. James did not have the required sums and was unable to comply with the order. I phoned a lawyer I knew who has an office within a two minute walk of the court house and asked him if he would go with James to the trial which would probable last no longer than five minutes. I let the attorney know the specifics of the case and he agreed that it was a slam dunk for James. James had told me he could borrow $500 to pay this attorney if he would only accompany him to the trial. The attorney told me $500 in this instance would not justify his time. James did not go to the final trial as he knew he didn't have a prayer with this judge even though Chapter 83 of the Florida Statutes supported his position 100%; plus he could not afford to lose another day's work. And he did not have the money required to appeal this judge's ruling to the appellate court. James was afraid he would be incarcerated for not paying as ordered. I informed James that the most the landlord could get was a judgment against him and since he had told me he had no assets, the landlord couldn't get blood out of a turnip. Garnishment of wages was out of the question as James is the head of the household. I told James to keep me apprised of any documentation he might receive from the court or the landlord. These courthouse folks have been known to take advantage of poor folks who are not familiar with the law even if it means violating the law. The judicial fraternity will do ANYTHING for a buck! I never heard any more from James.

Stories such as above are so numerous they alone could fill up a book.

GARNISHMENT

Garnishment is the satisfying of a legal debt, judgment or lien via an action through the judicial system whereby the debtor's funds (earnings, income, bank account, etc.) are given to the creditor or garnishor. The garnishee in a garnishment action is a third party (e.g. employer or bank) holding funds, assets or earnings of the defendant. The garnishor is the party or creditor to whom the defendant or debtor is indebted. Basically, all this means is that if you owe a dude and you don't pay him, he can come after you.

Garnishment is an exacting legal action and the procedures are specific and definitive. If you decide to affect garnishment on someone that legally owes you, do it right or it could come back to haunt you. First, make sure you sue him in the proper jurisdiction and get a judgment. The proper jurisdictions in my area are small claims court for issues up to $5,000, county court for issues up to $15,000, and circuit court for issues above $15,000. You are eligible to transfer to federal court on issues exceeding $50,000 but that action is beyond the scope of this book.

Once you have your final judgment, go to the court house and record it as soon as possible. Next make sure the debtor (dude that you have a recorded judgment against) has some net assets or is gainfully employed. If he is a deadbeat, broke and unemployed with no income, forget the effort and direct your energies elsewhere. You can't get blood out of a turnip, and they stopped putting folks in jail for debt in this country a couple of hundred years ago (except for child support and alimony). Incidentally, a garnishor (creditor) can get a pre-judgment garnishment but that won't be discussed here. Personal property other than salary and wages (bank accounts, stock accounts, etc.) can be garnished and the procedure is very similar but the example here will be based on garnishment of wages and salary. Every legal jurisdiction varies in their procedures so best to check with your local law library and clerk of the court before filing. In my jurisdiction in this example, once we had the final judgment, we then filed a Motion For Continuing Writ of Garnishment:

IN THE COUNTY COURT, IN AND FOR SEMINOLE COUNTY, FLORIDA

WINTER SPRINGS C. C.,   CASE NO. 98-308-SP-19-U
      Plaintiff,

vs

KOOL KAT,
      Defendant,

and

ROBBER AUTOMOTIVE AND TOWING, INC.,
      Garnishee.
_____/

PLAINTIFF'S MOTION FOR CONTINUING WRIT OF GARNISHMENT

Plaintiff, WINTER SPRINGS C. C., pursuant to § 77.0305, Florida Statutes, moves this Honorable Court for the issuance of a Continuing Writ of Garnishment, and as grounds therefore alleges as follows:

1. Plaintiff obtained a judgment against the Defendant on April 17, 1998 in the amount of $2,422.20, plus post judgment interest at 10%.

2. Plaintiff expects to recover the sum of:

Total amount of judgment	$2,422.20
Less payments against principal	00.00
Judgment balance	$2,422.20
Plus post judgment interest accruing at 10.00% on the principal amount of $2,422.20 through May 20, 19XX	21.89
Total amount claimed to date	$2,444.09

3. Plaintiff does not believe that the Defendant, KOOL KAT, has in his possession any visible property upon which a levy can be made sufficient to satisfy the judgment.

4. Plaintiff has reason to believe that the above named Garnishee has in its hands, possession or control, goods, salary or wages, bonus, commission, chattels, or effects belonging to the Defendant.

5. The property or thing sought to be garnished is not (1) wages for personal labor or services due the head of a family residing in the State of Florida; (2) the cash surrender value of life insurance policies issued upon the lives of citizens or residents of the State of Florida; or (3) disability income benefits due under a policy or contract of life, health, accident or other insurance.

WHEREFORE, Plaintiff moves this honorable Court to issue a Continuing Writ of Garnishment in this cause and tax the costs of the action against the Defendant.

DATED this _____ day of May, 20XX.

WINTER SPRINGS C. C., Plaintiff
By Dr. C. D. March, President
950 E. Highway 434
Winter Springs, Florida 32708
407-927-0494

Some jurisdictions require an Order For Continuing Writ Of Garnishment After Judgment while others just permit the Clerk of the Court to execute the Continuing Writ and have it served by the Sheriff:

IN THE COUNTY COURT, IN AND FOR SEMINOLE COUNTY, FLORIDA

WINTER SPRINGS C. C.,   CASE NO. 98-308-SP-19-U
    Plaintiff,

vs

KOOL KAT,
    Defendant,

and

ROBBER AUTOMOTIVE AND TOWING, INC.,
    Garnishee.

_____/

ORDER FOR CONTINUING WRIT OF GARNISHMENT AFTER JUDGMENT

THIS CAUSE coming before the Court on Motion of WINTER SPRINGS C. C. for Continuing Writ of Garnishment against salary and wages of the Defendant, KOOL KAT, and the Court being fully advised in the premises, it is thereupon

ORDERED and ADJUDGED that the Plaintiff, WINTER SPRINGS C. C., is entitled to, and shall have, a Continuing Writ of Garnishment against salary or wages of the Defendant, KOOL KAT.

DONE and ORDERED in chambers at Sanford, Seminole County, Florida, this _____ day of _____ , 2000.

_____
DLM, County Judge

You must present the Clerk of the Court with the Continuing Writ Of Garnishment Against Salary or Wages:

IN THE COUNTY COURT, IN AND FOR SEMINOLE COUNTY, FLORIDA

WINTER SPRINGS C. C.   CASE NO. 98-308-SP-19-U
     Plaintiff,

vs

KOOL KAT,
     Defendant,
and

ROBBER AUTOMOTIVE AND TOWING, INC.,
     Garnishee.
_____/

THE STATE OF FLORIDA
To Each Sheriff of the State:

YOU ARE COMMANDED to summon the garnishee, ROBBER AUTOMOTIVE AND TOWING, INC., whose address is 2500 Lake Drive, Atlas, Florida 32709, who is required to serve an answer to this writ on _____, 2000, to plaintiff whose address is 950 W. Highway 434, Winter Springs, Florida 32708, within 20 days after service of this writ, exclusive of the day of service, and to file the original with the clerk of the court either before service on the plaintiff or immediately thereafter. The answer shall state whether the garnishee is the employer of the defendant, KOOL KAT, and whither the garnishee is indebted to the defendant by reason of salary or wages. The garnishee's answer shall specify the periods of payment (for example, weekly, biweekly, or monthly) and amount of salary or wages and be based on the defendant's earnings for the pay period during which this writ is served on the garnishee.

During each pay period, a portion of the defendant's salary or wages as it becomes due shall be held and not disposed of or transferred until further order of this court. The amount of salary or wages to be withheld for each period shall be made in accordance with the following paragraph. This writ shall continue until the plaintiff's judgment is paid in full or until otherwise provided by court order. FEDERAL LAW (15 U. S. C. §§ 1671-1673) limits the amount to be withheld from salary or wages to no more than the amount by which the individual's disposable earnings for the pay period exceed 30 times the federal minimum hourly wage, whichever is less.

For administrative costs, the garnishee may collect $5.00 against salary or wages of the defendant for the first deduction and $2.00 for each deduction thereafter.

The total amount of the final judgment outstanding as set out in the plaintiff's motion is $2,422.20.

FAILURE TO FILE AN ANSWER WITHIN THE TIME REQUIRED MAY RESULT IN THE ENTRY OS JUDGMENT AGAINST THE GARNISHEE FOR THE ABOVE TOTAL AMOUNT OF $2,422.20.

ORDERED at Sanford, Seminole County, Florida, on the day of _____, 2000.

_____

MARYANNE MORSE
CLERK OF THE COURT

By _____
Deputy Clerk of the Court

The Continuing Writ Of Garnishment Against Salary or Wages is executed by either the county judge or the clerk of the court, depending on the local administrative rules. File all of the above documents with the Clerk of the Court at the same time. Filing and service of process fees vary. Service on the garnishee in Florida is not required by sheriff or certified process served but it is the best way to do it in order to avoid potential future problems.

Remember, if the debtor whose earnings you are garnishing is the "head of family", you can't or aren't supposed to garnish his disposable earnings which are less than or equal to $500 a week pursuant to Section 222.11, Florida Statutes. Better check with your particular state as to the "head of family" limitations. If the debtor does not declare "head of family" status as a defense, the court will undoubtedly rule in favor of the garnishor (creditor).

Here is a typical example of the legal fraternity sticking it to a Pro Se Litigant in a garnishment proceeding. This lady and her husband had a judgment recorded against them for non-payment of an unsecured loan with the local bank. The husband abandons the family and his whereabouts are unknown. The lady is gainfully employed and working, trying to keep what is left of the family together. She has a two year old baby and is 7 months pregnant (by her husband). The creditor bank files for garnishment of her employment earnings and her checking account at the local credit union. The defendant lady, not being able to afford a lawyer, is unsuccessful in combating the bank's attorneys who are successful in court and initiate the appropriate garnishment proceedings against this young mother. About ten months after the garnishment actions were in force, this lady came to us for help. After perusing all of her documents I questioned her to ascertain that she was the "head of family" as defined by Section 222.11(a), Florida Statutes. "Head of family' includes any natural person who is providing more than one-half of the support for a child or other dependent." She definitely qualified for "head of family" status. I asked her if any of the bank's attorneys or the judge asked her if she were the "head of family" and she replied "no". She did not know to declare this fact at the hearing. Technically the judge was letting the bank's attorneys garnish this lady's pay and checking account illegally. Immediately we filed a motion to stop this outrageous ruling.

MOTION TO SET ASIDE GARNISHMENT

Defendant moves the court pursuant to Fla. R. Civ. P. 1.540, to set aside the Writ of Garnishment and Continuing Writ of Garnishment entered in the above-styled action on December nth, 19xx, on the ground that the pleadings herein affirmatively show no claim in fact exists against Defendant, in that

1. "No writ of attachment of garnishment or other process shall issue from any of the courts of this state to attach or delay the payment of any money or other thing due to any person who is head of a family residing in this state, when the money or other thing is due for personal labor or other services of such person." Section 222.11, Florida Statutes.

2. The effect of this Motion To Set Aside is to return the parties to the position they occupied before the garnishment was entered. Zwakhals v. Senft, 206 So. 2d (Fla. 4th DCA 1968).

3. Pursuant to Section 222.11, Florida Statutes, SALLY GOODIE, Defendant, is hereby the "head of family".

WHEREFORE, by reason of the above, SALLY GOODIE, respectfully moves this Honorable Court to set aside the Writ of Garnishment and Continuing Writ of Garnishment entered on December nth, 19xx, and deny Order For Continuing Writ of Garnishment After Judgment and return the parties to the position they occupied before the Writ of Garnishment and Continuing Writ of Garnishment were executed.

DATED ON this _____ day of _____, 20yy.

_____

SALLY GOODIE, Defendant/Pro Se Litigant

(Once again the caption and certificate of service are omitted from the motion to preclude redundancy.)

It would be wise to make the above motion verified or else submit an affidavit with it affirming the stated facts. The above motion was filed at the court house, a copy mailed to the bank's attorneys and the defendant was able to get a hearing date for it. As procedurally required, she mailed out the appropriate hearing notice to the bank's attorneys and filed the original of the notice with the court. Her hearing was scheduled for 10:30 A.M. She had to take the day off work for the hearing and at noon that day I received a phone call from this young lady and she was crying. She said, "The bank had two attorney's arguing against me and we beat them." Talk about making my day! The Court had ordered the bank to reimburse her all funds taken under the garnishment action. A victory, yes, but not a total victory yet. I figured the scumbag attorneys would still try to jerk this little lady around some more and I was right. The judge had given the attorneys four days to have an order per the above motion on his desk for signature. Two weeks passed and the bank's lawyers still didn't have the order in front of the judge as had been ordered. We filed a Motion For Contempt as follows:

MOTION FOR CONTEMPT

COMES NOW Defendant, SALLY GOODIE, and files this Motion For Contempt and in support thereof says:

1. At 10:30 A.M., Monday, the nth day of September, 20yy, this honorable Court heard the Defendant's Motion To Set Aside Garnishment and granted same.

2. This Court ordered the Plaintiff's attorney, JOE JERKOFF, to write the order setting aside garnishment and returning the parties to the position they occupied before the garnishment was entered and to have said order in Judge Money Bags' chambers no later than Friday, September vth, 20yy.

3. The Plaintiff's attorney, JOE JERKOFF, has failed to obey this Court's order and this violation is causing the Defendant undue financial hardship. Defendant can not enjoy release of her garnished funds until the Honorable Judge Money Bags signs subject order and Defendant receives a copy of the executed order.

WHEREFORE, the Defendant, SALLY GOODIE, moves this honorable Court for its order finding the Plaintiff's attorney, JOE JERKOFF, in willful contempt of this Court's order of September nth, 19yy, and for such sanctions as this Court deems appropriate under the circumstances.

DATED at Seminole County, Florida this _____ day of _____, 20yy.

_____
SALLY GOODIE, Defendant/Pro Se Litigant

Three days after the young lady filed the above contempt motion with the court, she had on her desk an order executed by the judge and a check reimbursing her all previous funds taken by the bank under the writ of garnishment. Sometimes even lawyers are made to obey court orders in due time... We charged the young lady $95 for this entire episode.

I would like to make a point here that the above case is not a rare occurrence by any means. We've had a number of similar cases. The legal fraternity just doesn't give a damn about the folks in this country that can't afford legal representation in court. And those in the profession that deny this fact are damn liars.

Let me tell you about a garnishment case that did not turn out as well for a lady who was 62 years old. She was earning $440 a month as a maid in a nursing home. She was a nice person but definitely not a rocket scientist. She took care of and was the sole support of her 81 year old mother. Her mother had diabetes, blind, and numerous other physical problems. This lady came to me with the problem that the bank was garnishing her wages and she literally did not have any money to live on. Coming under the definition of "head of family", I immediately had her file a Motion To Set Aside Garnishment and a Notice of Hearing with the Clerk of the Court. Needless to say, this was another pro bono case. At the hearing the county judge took testimony from the bank's attorney via telephone. The lady had been given no fore warning of this telephonic hearing which is a blatant violation of the Florida Rules of Civil Procedure. The Rules state that you must inform and get approval from the other side and the judge before having a telephonic hearing. The judge denied the lady's petition with no reason, period. She had attended the hearing by herself which I warned her not to do. You see, judges will take advantage of pro se litigants that come to a hearing without anyone or without a court reporter. It's the judge's word against yours and your word doesn't mean a damn thing in a situation like this. The judge realizes this little old lady isn't going to contribute to his re-election campaign fund, but that lawyer probably will. And the judge doesn't want to be bothered by this little old lady's financial problems. As anticipated, the judge ruled against this lady in violation of her constitutional rights and Florida Statutes. I heard no more from this lady and therefore was not able to further help her in a possible appeal.

E. D. came to me about an attorney trying to garnish her wages from a judgment entered on her a goodly number of years ago. I would guess E. D. to be about 60 years old. She works as a receptionist at the local hash house. She has two legal dependents besides herself, her daughter and her granddaughter. All dependents have been legally declared on her federal income tax return for the past three years. She informed me that if they garnished the $127 a month so stipulated in the Continuing Writ of Garnishment, she would not be able to pay her rent and she and the girls would be thrown out into the street.

Both Florida law and federal law prohibit garnishment of one's wages who is the "head of family household." A first year law student is cognizant of this fact. I filed a Motion To Set Aside Garnishment with a Memorandum of Law quoting state and federal case law supporting E.D.s position. Judge C. denied the motion! I then filed a Motion For Summary Judgment with affidavit and other appropriate documents. The judge again denied! Once again, I reiterate that the judicial fraternity just doesn't give a damn about a pro se litigant. The court will blatantly violate the law when no one is watching over them. This has been and is being proven everyday in the courts of this country. Just because this lady did not have an attorney representing her nor a court reporter transcribing what was going on, the judge threw her to the dogs. Hell, the judge is up for re-election this year and that lady isn't going to contribute any funds to the judge's campaign. But the plaintiff's attorney very well might   Note what happens next in this case..

Since I could not represent this lady in court, I reluctantly used up one of my IOUs and called on an attorney I know in town to handle this case pro bono. It was a slam dunk with an attorney representing E. D. The attorney used the same documents I had already submitted excepting that he added his name to them. The judge then affirmed the setting aside of the Writ of Continuing Garnishment. I tend to see this sort of discrimination against Pro Se Litigants on a daily basis in the judicial system and it really upsets me.

Now let's get back to where we filed all of the garnishment documents as previously shown and the garnishee was served by the sheriff. The garnishee (debtor's employer) has 20 days from the day of service in which to answer the summons. If the garnishee does not answer, then he, the garnishee, could be held liable for the debt. You have five days from the time you receive an answer from the garnishee to send copies of all of the filed papers plus the answer to the debtor. Then you must file the Notice of Continuing Writ of Garnishment with a Certificate of Service. Should either the garnishee or the debtor hire an attorney during the course of this action, I would strongly advise you doing the same. Garnishment laws are very specific and the monetary penalty for violating them could be significant. Under normal conditions you should start getting your judgment moneys from the garnishee soon thereafter.

Make sure you know what you are doing in a garnishment procedure. Follow the procedure precisely. If the debtor or garnishee hire an attorney to represent them and they are successful in voiding or overturning your writ of garnishment, you in all likelihood will be responsible for their legal fees and costs.

RECUSAL (DISQUALIFICATION) OF JUDGES

Recusal or disqualification as it pertains to presiding judges is more or less self-explanatory. It means just what it says. The major reason for the implementation of recusal of a judge in a legal process (trial or hearing) is to preclude any degree of alleged prejudice by the presiding judge. Recusal can be either voluntary or involuntary. The judge may recuse himself. If so, the parties usually accept this self-disqualification. Or one or both of the parties may initiate a Motion For Recusal or Disqualification for a myriad of reasons. Rarely does a presiding judge recuse himself. Judges consider themselves the brothers of King Solomon in knowledge (of everything legal and otherwise) and beyond any possible prejudicial feelings whatsoever.

When the need to file a Motion For Recusal arises, the filer must have substantial basis for this action. You can not successfully initiate such an action because you don't like the way the judge looks or talks or any other such ridiculous reason. The statutes and rules of judicial procedure in these matters are very finite and usually have good case law supporting them. When filing a Motion For Recusal of a sitting judge, always do it on the basis that you will have to appeal his decision as in many cases your motion will be denied. Will the appellate court overturn his decision? Yes, if you have done your homework and can substantiate your fear of being denied due process or justice by this particular judge.

Once the judge has made his decision in your case, it is too late to file for recusal. You must initiate this action before he renders his decision. Again, it goes without saying, if you do not have a court reporter at your hearing or trial to substantiate your accusations, it is the judge's word against yours and, my friend, you don't stand a chance. This may not be true if there are certain mitigating circumstances having occurred before the hearing involving you and the judge in some manner or other. My advice...have a court reporter.

I have had two judges recused. In the first instance the judge was hearing a contempt charge on the former husband for non-payment of alimony. It was ironical in that the former wife was living in a 5,000 square foot house and had a salary three times that of the former husband. This poor client could not afford a lawyer and yet the legal system wanted him to pay alimony. The former wife's attorney requested a multitude of documents from the former husband for discovery purposes. Actually it was nothing but a harassing and fishing expedition inasmuch as the attorney needed to build up some hours for legal fees. The former husband informed the attorney that he really didn't have a lot of actual records (canceled checks, etc.) but would give the attorney written permission to acquire any and all of his financial records in financial institutions, the IRS, or any other entity the attorney so desired. The attorney became upset at this and told the former husband, "We'll see what Solomon has to say about this!" Solomon, by the way, was the judge's first name. We knew right then that we were going to file for recusal. On further investigation, I found out through research in the appellate level that Solomon was having an affair with this female attorney of the former wife. That appeal was the basis for a successful recusal at the appellate level overturning Solomon's recusal denial involving another case before him where this same female attorney was representing one of the parties before Solomon. Isn't justice great.

In the second recusal in which I was involved, we were just lucky to have a transcript from a prior hearing in front of this judge who castigated my client. My client was not a party in the action involving said transcript nor even present at that hearing. But the judge, as many judges do, had made some disparaging personal remarks about my client pursuant to some work he had done that was vaguely involved in that case but should not have even been brought to light. Subsequently, my client was scheduled for hearing before this judge on a contempt motion in a different action. We knew this judge was gunning for my client and that the judge would probably incarcerate him. We filed a Motion For Recusal and supported our accusations for fear of being subjected to a biased judge with the aforementioned transcript. The judge stated that he would have gladly recused himself had he known the client's feelings and that the client did not have to include the transcript in his motion. Yea, sure. Had we not included the transcript the judge would have denied the motion, we would have had no hard evidentiary basis for appeal and the judge would have enjoyed sending my client to jail. A different judge was assigned and after the contempt hearing my client did not go to jail.

Again, make sure you have a sound, substantive basis for trying to recuse a judge. Case law is full of cites giving acceptable grounds for recusal.

RULES OF CIVIL PROCEDURE

The Rules of Civil Procedure are endemic to the legal system as a way to establish order and systematic organization. It is supposed to keep the system in some semblance of order and continuity. These rules are like the grease that keeps the legal wheel running smoothly and not squeak. In a way it is similar to Robert's Rules of Order in maintaining order and definition during such formal meetings as corporate meetings, director meetings, governmental meetings. Nevertheless, former U. S. Supreme Court Chief Justice Warren Burger once said, "Lawyers have a way of papering their profession with 'rules' which are advisory, vague and widely ignored." These rules are voluminous and only a rare attorney or judge is familiar with all of them. A relatively limited number of the rules are utilized a majority of the time by Pro Se Litigants. I will try to address those rules most commonly used. Please remember, I am not an attorney and the views I am expressing are my layman's opinion. Incidentally, if you can walk and chew gum at the same time, you will be able to go to your local law library and peruse a copy of your State Rules of Civil Procedure and decipher them. The index will guide you to a wealth of information in the area in which you are interested.

In addition to the Rules of Civil Procedure, there are situations where certain administrative rules are disseminated in local jurisdictions effecting only the local courts. When in a local jurisdiction, one must obey not only the State Rules of Civil Procedure but also the local administrative policies, rules and procedures. The local rules can vary substantially from one jurisdiction to another within the same state. In reality, these local guidelines are usually made up by certain of the judges in any local jurisdiction as a method of saying, "Boys, if you're going to play on our field, you'd better do it exactly like we local boys say do it". Usually the local administrative policies, rules and procedures guidelines can be obtained by nicely asking the Clerk of the Court for a copy of them. Be careful around the deputy Clerks in the court house as they are part of the legal fraternity. I will go more into depth on that one later.

Sometimes the local administrative rules violate the law. In Orange County all pro se litigants filing for a dissolution of marriage (divorce) must have their documents approved on the 8th floor of the court house before they can file them. Case law dictates that the Clerk of the Court is a ministerial position and the Clerk must accept documents for filing. However, they repeatedly turn pro se litigants away from filing for divorce, telling them their papers are not proper and they should get an attorney. We have our clients demand of the Clerks that they accept their papers for filing...and they do, both the Clerks and our clients. The vast majority of pro se litigants filing for uncontested (and contested) divorces are easily intimidated in this court house environment as they do not know the rules or procedures. The legal fraternity will do anything to enhance their financial troughs and they really don't give a damn whether or not a pro se litigant can afford their services.

One of the important procedural rules of which one must be aware is that regarding timeliness. When served a summons you have a finite number of days in which to reply or as the legal connotation says, answer. In Florida, for example, when one (usually respondent) is served with a Petition for Dissolution Marriage, the person served the petition has twenty (20) days from the date of service to answer the allegations in the petition. An answer usually contains affirmations, denials, and/or without knowledge as to each allegation in the petition. An answer can also incorporate a counter-petition and/or affirmative defenses into it following the answer section, if so desired by defendant. Basically the counter-petition reiterates some of the factual statements from the petition and then requests from the court certain relief (what the defendant/respondent wants). It is wise in these initial pleadings for both plaintiff and defendant to ask of the court for attorney fees and costs. If you don't ask initially, odds are it won't be considered by the court later. Even if you are representing yourself, ask for fees and costs as you might end up requiring legal representation from an attorney before it's all over.

Your twenty day time limit expires and you haven't answered the petition. The plaintiff can file a motion for default with the Clerk of the Court. This means any subsequent answer you try to file with the court relating to this petition can be and should be denied as not being timely. If the other side has an attorney representing them, the judge will almost always set aside your default in order for the attorney to answer the petition. The discretionary power of the judge is practically unlimited. He has the authoritative discretion to accept an untimely answer. If the plaintiff doesn't like it, the judge's philosophy to the plaintiff is, "Go ahead and appeal my decision to the (Florida) District Court of Appeals". Of course, an appeal will probably cost the plaintiff $5,000 to $25,000 in legal fees plus costs and prolong his action another 6 to 18 months. And then there is the ire of the judge whose decision you appealed which you have to endure for the balance of your case when it comes back from the District Court of Appeals, regardless of whether you won or lost on the appellate level. When they tell you that your appeal does not bother the judge or effect his subsequent decisions regarding your case, don't believe it.

Some rare judges realize you are a Pro Se Litigant and that the United States Supreme Court has held that you are not to be held on the same technical plane as an attorney and therefore, will accept your untimely answer. But don't try to take advantage of the system or this amenable judge might just decide to cut your feet out from under you before it's over. And if the other side is being represented by a lawyer and you are representing yourself, most of the time the judge will rule against you even if the law supports your case. Don't like it? Then appeal, says the judge. Now is a good time to tell you what one judge once told me. He said, "Say there are two attorneys in court in front of me and one represents the plaintiff and one represents the defendant and I personally know these two attorneys. And say one of the attorneys is very prepared for his case and the law supports his position while the other attorney is ill-prepared and really doesn't know what the

167

hell he is doing. Say I consider the well prepared attorney a real jerk and I have great disdain for him while the other attorney is a friend of mine or one of the good ole boys. If the ill-prepared, good ole boy will just give me a minute, minuscule, inconsequential cite or reason to rule in his client's favor, I will do so. If the well prepared attorney doesn't like it, appeal. Hell, he'll make more money in legal fees if he can convince his client to appeal regardless of whether nor not he wins the appeal." My advice to a Pro Se Litigant in a similar situation is like Texas Bix Bender once said, "If you find yourself in a hole, the first thing to do is stop diggin'".

I figure by now that you are starting to get the point that it's a court of law and not a court of justice. Justice doesn't have a damn thing to do with it.

After your answer has been filed, the discovery process usually begins. If any attorneys are involved, they will churn the system during the discovery process in an effort to generate additional legal fees. Basically, discovery is the process where you may legally, ask questions, request certain documents (federal tax returns, notes, bank account files, anything to do with assets and liabilities) of the opposing party, pursue anything that is not privileged that might aid you in your case. However, what is good for the goose is also good for the gander. The other party can require the same of you.

Interrogatories are part of the discovery process. Interrogatories are usually written questions requesting certain information. They are timely in that you generally have 30 to 45 days in which to respond. If you feel the questions are not important to the case or the other party is just trying to harass you, you can file a motion for protection. This motion can be for the entire interrogatory or just specific questions in it. This is a hearing motion and you must get a date and time from the judge's secretary for the hearing and inform the other side in writing accordingly. Remember to include a fully written Order with any motion you file with the court. Neither the judge nor his assistant have time to write your orders for you and they will appreciate your conscientiousness. Also include two stamped, self-addressed envelopes (one for you, the other for the opposing side) with the proposed order so that the judge's secretary doesn't have to do it. After the judge signs the order, following your hearing, copies are mailed out to the respective parties. The content of the order you submit is based on the assumption that the judge rules in your favor.

Included under discovery is the motion to produce. This is where the other party or his attorney requests that you bring certain documents to his place for his perusal and copying. Again you can file a motion for protection under the same criteria as stated above. In some states you can require the party that filed the motion to produce to come to where you have the requested documents if located in a different county than where the documents are located. Check your Rules of Civil Procedure.

Under discovery the other party can file a motion for production by a third party. A good example of this is your adversary wanting your employer to produce your salary or pay check stubs for the past year. Usually you must be informed of the other party's intent to file a motion for production by a third party ten or so days before the third party is actually served. The reason for this timely notice is to give you ample opportunity to file for a protective order (motion for protection) to try and stop this action. You may not want your employer knowing what is going on and/or the data and/or information requested by the other party may not be relevant and is just harassment. You also have the right to file a motion for production from a third party.

Attorneys can really build up their fees during the discovery process with motions to compel, motions to protect, motions for production from third parties, motions only limited by your imagination. There are certain things you can do to drive the other party up a wall and increase his legal fees during discovery such as denying you have all of the canceled checks, federal tax returns, etc. that are requested of you. Then in an effort to cooperate, give the other party letters of authorization for him to retrieve this data and information from the respective sources, e.g. Internal Revenue Service, financial institutions. Unless it's a substantial case involving significant sums of money or assets, or an irate wife/husband, they won't pursue your financial history past your financial affidavit. Be advised, if they do go to great lengths to uncover the aforementioned financial data and/or information, the judge has the discretion to assess you for all costs incurred by them. Just remember that in today's environment of Big Brother, it's real easy to trace any and all assets and other germane information on an individual. Computers are great for this. I have seen attorneys make a big deal out of the discovery process, knowing full well that you don't have any assets, just to create additional billable hours to enhance their legal fees.

Admissions is another nicety in discovery that can save you time and money. These are questions or statements which are relevant to the action at hand, submitted to the other party in printed form, requesting that they agree or admit that the given statement(s) is true or correct. Usually, here as with interrogatories and production, the other party can file a motion for protection. However, they usually admit or deny the statement. The admitted statements are then part of the record and don't have to be argued during the trial.

Discovery is a very important part of the judicial process. Sometimes enough incriminating evidence comes forth in discovery as to bring the action to a conclusion via a motion to dismiss, summary judgment, voluntary dismissal, etc. and not having to go to trial.

Motions are the bane of the client and the Jaguar and airplane payments for the attorney. As previously stated, motions are only limited by one's imagination. There are motions to dismiss with prejudice and without prejudice (can bring the cause back up again either amended or whatever), motions to abate, motions for continuance, motions for protection,and on and on and on. Just remember, certain motions require substantive add on criteria. Some motions must be verified. Some motions require an affidavit. Some motions, like a motion to recuse (disqualify) a judge are timely and are not valid if filed with the court after a time certain. Although motions tend to be a necessary element in the judicial process lawyers are infamous for using them needlessly to prolong an action (case) and thereby justify additional billable hours and legal fees.

After discovery, and sometimes during discovery, usually a pre-trial conference is set up. This is where the parties to the action meet with the judge to ascertain the guidelines or ground rules for the trial and the admissibility of evidence in addition to any other important factors which might be brought up at trial. This hearing is usually very informal and takes place in the judge's chambers. Subsequent to the pre-trial conference, if there is one, the action or cause goes to trial.

The above procedures have been discussed in a very general nature and represent an extremely limited number of the actual procedures. Your state may vary somewhat in its procedures. But the fact remains that the State Rules of Civil Procedure are the backbone of the judicial process in your jurisdiction and volumes have been written about them. The Rules of Criminal Procedure are a different species altogether and are not germane to this book.

Let's briefly discuss local administrative rules, policies and procedural guidelines. As previously stated, these guidelines are local in nature and are usually in addition to the Rules of Civil Procedure. As an example, let's look at the "Administrative Policies And Procedures Guidelines" put out by the Civil/Family Division of the Eighth Judicial Circuit Court, In and For Lake County, Florida. There are four circuit judges in this Division. They are Judge SB, Judge NB, Judge AD and Judge TF. These Guidelines consist of nineteen pages and the index. The index is broken down as follows:

Judge SB was the prime author of these administrative guidelines. He put a lot of work into them and theoretically they are ideal. Realistically most of these guidelines are ridiculous. On the reverse side of the coin, however, certain of these guidelines are time saving devices that function well. Throughout these guidelines are statements such as, "PLEASE SEE APPENDIX 'A' FOR FURTHER REQUIREMENTS BY JUDGE SB AND JUDGE NB" and "JUDGE SB AND JUDGE NB WILL REQUIRE THE FOLLOWING CERTIFICATION:...........JUDGE AD AND JUDGE TF DO NOT REQUIRE THIS CERTIFICATION" and "JUDGE SB AND JUDGE NB THE FOLLOWING WILL APPLY:..........JUDGE AD AND JUDGE TF DO NOT REQUIRE THE ABOVE CERTIFICATION." Judge AD and Judge TF apparently realize the true nature of these guidelines. In many instances they tend to form a needless bureaucratic bottleneck in the judicial process thereby increasing the cost of so-called justice to the average Joe Six-pack. For example, let's look at the Pre-trial Conference guideline. In a non-contested dissolution of marriage (divorce) where there are no minors nor any assets involved, the parties must attend a pre-trial conference! Why? Who knows. There is absolutely nothing to discuss under these conditions at the pre-trial conference. All it does is force the parties to lose a day from work to attend a pre-trial conference that will last a minute. Perhaps it makes the judge feel powerful in being able to exercise such authority over average Joe Six-pack. Incidentally, many of my clients have had to needlessly lose a day from work because of this. What's even more devastating to the average Pro Se Litigant who had to take the day off work is to appear at a hearing or pre-trial conference only to be told that it was canceled. The judicial assistant usually says, "Weren't you notified?" Unless you're an attorney, the system could care less about you.

Finally, you're at trial and the Rules of Civil Procedure still control. There is only one thing that supersedes the Rules of Civil Procedure at the trial and that's the judge. He is like unto God in his domain, the court room. The judge has full, unabashed authority in the court room. His actions and orders are beyond question while in the court room during trial. Although some attorneys do question the judge during trial, don't believe for one minute that the judge doesn't file that comment away in the back of his mind for future reference. The judge's philosophy is, "If you don't like my decision, appeal it." Like attorneys, many judges are incompetent. Like police officers, many judges have an ego problem and do not want to be questioned on any of their actions. Similar to elected politicians who initially go into office with visions of grandeur, many judges soon become part of the system. And believe me, the system is not there to help out the poor dumb litigant that can't afford an attorney. I know, I deal within the judicial system everyday.

I trust you now realize how important the State Rules of Civil Procedure are in your case. Unless your action involves serious money or assets or you're in an adversarial posture involving custody of the children you really want, you can probably go it alone as a Pro Se Litigant. I would advise you to consider the help of a competent independent paralegal, however. And remember, if the other side has an attorney representing them, the court system in all likelihood is going to treat you, a Pro Se Litigant, like dirt.

WILLS, TRUSTS AND PROBATE

This subject matter generates billions of dollars annually into the coffers of the legal fraternity. This is in fact the proverbial "license to steal" and do the judges and lawyers ever know it.

First, let's define the above terms in a layman's definition. Wills (last will and testament) and trusts (revocable living trust) are instruments whereby one gives, bequeaths and/or devises his assets to certain individuals (beneficiaries) upon his death or demise. The legal process by which these assets are distributed is called probate. These are rather simplistic definitions as books have been written on the subject.

Simple wills, which probably constitute 70 - 80% of the written Last Will and Testaments in this country, can usually be written by the individual or an independent paralegal. Be careful though, as your particular state may have some hidden hookers in the law whereby the lawyers are the only ones that can write a legal last will and testament. Usually the lawyers try to get the legislature (which in many cases is predominately made up of lawyers) to sneak in laws that cover them financially. For instance, you must have an attorney for probate purposes unless you are the only beneficiary and are knowledgeable enough to work your way through the quagmire of bureaucratic paper work and legal documents. Additionally, in Florida by law you must have an attorney if you want to generate a guardianship. You are supposed to have an attorney if you want a Revocable Living Trust. I know of lawyers that can't even spell trust let alone draw one up properly. Yet they can legally author such a document for the public. It would be funny if it weren't so pitiful.

A simple will, often referred to as a Last Will and Testament, usually means you are leaving your assets to your spouse if you predecease her or else to your biological children or whoever. You can not cut your spouse entirely out of your will in Florida. The spouse is due at least an elective share (30%) if the surviving spouse so elects. Homestead plays a very significant part in distribution of one's assets in Florida, also. If you are not sure of what you are doing and can not find a competent independent paralegal, I strongly recommend you go to an attorney that is board certified in probate in your state to draw up your will. You will pay a premium but in this instance it may well be worth it.

The testator's (person for whom the will is made) signature being witnessed by two competent, non-related, adults, on a properly drawn up last will and testament is usually legal and binding. However, I always recommend that the signatures of the testator and both witnesses be notarized. This is known as self-proofing a will. If the witnesses' signatures are not notarized, the judge at probate could require the personal appearance of the two witnesses to affirm the fact that the signature on the will is that of the testator. What if both or either of the witnesses is deceased or unavailable? Boy, lawyers love that scenario. It means more billable hours, more money for the legal beagles, less assets for the estate and kids. Now you've got to prove to the judge's discretionary satisfaction that the testator's signature on the will is really the testator's signature.

If you have minor children, don't forget to incorporate into your last will and testament terminology regarding who has authority to act as guardian of the minor children after the parents' demise. Also, who is going to be the trustee for the estate assets which are bequeathed to the minors? And how and when do you want these assets distributed to the minor children? It's all very important and should be outlined in your will very specifically. The more specific and definitive your last will and testament, the less chance of some greedy attorney talking an interested party into contesting the will and having grounds accordingly. Contested wills are financial smorgasbords for the legal brethren. The probate judge usually will aid the local attorney in any possible (and sometimes impossible) way to prolong probate of the estate and drag it out. You got it...more billable hours. If you think I'm pulling your leg, just ask any of your friends who have gone through the probate experience their opinion of the process and the legal fraternity associated with it.

Two years ago an elderly widow came to us to help her in probate of her husband's estate who had just passed away. She was naive as to the ways of the legal profession and was absolutely appalled at some of the financial quotes she was getting from lawyers on the probate of her deceased husband's small estate. Since she was the only beneficiary, Florida Statute said she could legally do the probate without an attorney. Not counting her homestead (a mobile home worth about $25,000), the probate estate had a value of less than $10,000. We agreed to help her. The Florida Legal Secretary publication outlines exactly what to do in this case. All of the proper documents were filed with the probate court in Orange County, Florida. The judge, who historically had been known to deny Pro Se Litigants any relief, denied this elderly widow in this probate cause saying in his order, "...until proper compliance has been made with the applicable Florida Statutes and Rules of Probate and Guardianship Procedure...." Baloney! He knew damn well the documents filed were impeccable and legally proper but wanted the legal fraternity to get its just due out of the estate. We had charged this lady $50 for the paper work which we ended up reimbursing her. We sadly told her that she had the option of appeal to the 5th District Court of Appeals where I never had any doubt but that the judge would be overturned or hire some sleaze-bag attorney. In an effort to get it over with and behind her as soon as possible she hired an attorney who charged her $1,800 and took 6 months. Oh, by the way, the attorney's documents were identical to those originally filed by the pro se litigant.

Probate costs vary from state to state. Usually they are a percentage of the probate estate. Sounds simple and easy, doesn't it? For sake of discussion, let's say the cost of probate (fees for the probate attorney) is a typical 6% of the gross estate. Exactly what does that mean? Say, for instance, the only asset in the estate is a $100,000 house and there is a first mortgage on this house of $90,000. And the only creditors of the estate are the funeral home ($3,000) and probate legal fees. You don't have to be a rocket scientist to figure out that the

Legal Whores

attorney gets $6,000 (6% X $100,000 gross) of the net $10,000 available
for distribution and the funeral home gets $3,000. The balance of this
estate is $1,000 which sum is now distributed to the beneficiaries as
directed in the will by the dead dude. The law in Florida directs that
assets in an estate are to be paid out (distributed) in this **order: (1)
lawyer fees and court costs,** (2) funeral expenses, (3) taxes, (4) medical
and hospital expenses, (5) family allowance, (6) arrearage from court
ordered child support, (7) business debts acquired after the decedent's
death, (8) all other claims.[73] Please note what position the probate
attorney is in. Right on: the attorney gets paid before anyone or
anything else. Do these dudes cover their asses or what...

Most folks erroneously believe that having a last will and
testament avoids the probate process and thereby unconscionable legal
fees. Wrong. If a person dies with a will (testate) or without a will
(intestate), their estate is probated. How do you avoid probate? There
are a number of ways but I will discuss the more common. I figure if
you have a few million dollar estate you can and should afford the
services of a competent, board certified attorney.

Firstly, having a revocable living trust instead of a last will and
testament usually avoids probate in Florida. Better check with your
particular jurisdiction. I will discuss revocable living trusts in more
detail later. Owning personal and/or real property jointly with rights of
survivorship can avoid probate. Personal property includes such things
as your vehicle, stocks, household contents, etc.: real property relates to
real estate like your home. Realize, however, that homestead (the
marital residence) can be somewhat of a different situation for a married
couple. Joint ownership means the deed or title or whatever
conveyance document there is, states on it the names of the individuals
with the word or between the names and following all names the
terminology joint tenancy with right of survivorship. Everyone involved
here is considered to be an adult. If children are involved, it can be a
different story. When one of the joint owners dies, his share
automatically is equally divided among the survivor owners in joint

[73] Section 733.707, Florida Statutes

178

tenancy. Even if he had willed his share to someone else, the joint tenancy with right of survivorship takes precedence. One caveat to this method of avoiding probate is that if one of the owners (joint tenants) has a judgment placed on himself individually, it might detrimentally effect the whole of subject property as a lien, title cloud or encumbrance.

A simple note of interest about the executor, now called personal representative in Florida, who is the entity (person, corporation) in the will or trust that is responsible for administration of the document. If the personal representative lives outside of your state of residence, he should be a blood relative. Otherwise, it doesn't matter unless your particular state dictates differently. Common sense directs that the personal representative should be someone who lives in the same general locale as you. Think about it. It is better if the personal representative is not a beneficiary. Sometimes this is not possible though. Incidentally, do you know why lawyers want to keep your original will in their offices? At your death where do your survivors go? They go to the attorney who has your original will and he ends up being the attorney of record for the probate process. Talk about a captive market.

Another method of probate avoidance is a revocable living trust, not to be confused with a living will or last will and testament. The revocable living trust is a compilation of documents whereby your wishes for distribution of your assets, in addition to other possible requests, are subscribed. It is not usually subject to formal probate administration through the courts. The big advantages of a revocable living trust over a will are probate avoidance, lower administrating cost, more expeditious in administering and privacy. By the way, if your intent is to cut your spouse out of even the statutorily required elective share (minimum 30%) via a last will and testament, the revocable living trust might be the way to accomplish this feat. In the probate process a last will and testament is of public record while this is not so with a revocable living trust. In Florida, the lawyers made sure through the state legislature in 1993 that they could still get their greedy little hands on some of the trust estate via the new Section 733.617, Florida Statue whereby a mandatory personal representative fee based on the probated inventory value of the estate must be paid. Needless to say, the lawyers want to be your personal representative. The only saving grace here is that the personal representative does not have to be an attorney...yet.

Federal and state tax consequences are not being discussed here. Suffice to say that estates are entitled to a $600,000 exemption from federal taxes. The Congress has stated that this will increase as a function of time. If your estate is valued in excess of this amount, I strongly advise you to seek the advice of a competent, board certified probate attorney. Shop around for a good attorney and compare costs. Speaking of costs, independent paralegals normally charge $50 for a simple will for an individual and $80 for a married couple. Lawyers usually charge $400 to $750 for the same thing. Revocable living trusts can cost from $250 for individuals and $350 for a married couple when done by independent paralegals. Attorneys will try to get from $700 to $5,000 or whatever they think the traffic will bear.

Some folks do not need to waste their money on a revocable living trust instead of a last will and testament. Avoiding probate via a trust if your assets are in a five figure range (e.g. around $100,000 or less) is really not financially smart. Figure out the probate cost (legal fees and administration) in your state versus the cost of a revocable living trust relative to the size of your estate. In the central Florida area is a 466 lot mobile home park. Many of these fine, elderly folks are my clients. I usually talk them out of my doing a revocable living trust for them because their assets tend to be such that a last will and testament will suffice for what they need. And since the legislature recently passed a law forbidding non-lawyers from doing trusts, I can no longer do them anyway. I must share with you what recently occurred at this mobile home park. The mobile home park was a rental park until last year when the owners sold the individual lots to the respective tenants (mobile home owners). The attorney for the sellers of the park told the 466 lot purchasers that since they were now owners of their respective lots, they should each have a revocable living trust to protect their assets. He personally guaranteed them a one time cost of $750 each only for them. The attorney assured them he would expedite their revocable living trusts on a first come, first served basis. According to my arithmetic, this lawyer was looking to gross a quick $350.000. All he does is turn this project over to his $8.00 an hour secretary who has the basic revocable living trust format already in the computer. Based on my experience, the secretary can bang out a simple trust every 30 minutes. So you figure 466 revocable trusts at 30 minutes per trust takes 233 man hours at $8.00 per hour is less than $4,000, if you include overhead. When you look at $350,000 income for a $4,000 outgo, no wonder every Tom, Dick and Harry wants to become a lawyer and why we are inundated with this breed in America.

Other documents which should be given consideration when having a will prepared are living will, power of attorney and health surrogate form. These important documents can be explained to you by the preparer of your last will and testament or trust and will not be discussed here.

Legal Whores

WRITS

Writs are a court's written order to do or refrain from doing some specified act. There are a number of different writs but I will only discuss those that can be and are utilized the most. Most lawyers usually don't use writs because they are not familiar with them and really don't understand them.

According to the 7th Edition of Black's Law Dictionary, the writ of mandamus is a writ issued by a superior court to compel a lower court or a government officer to perform mandatory or purely ministerial duties correctly. Following are some examples of what this means.

In some states there is a rule where the court must resolve your divorce within a 180 day time limit unless there are certain prevailing mitigating circumstances. In such a scenario, if you are a Pro Se Litigant, say in a marital cause, and the court and/or its personnel are jerking your chain time-wise even though all of your paperwork is proper and timely, you may file a Petition for Writ of Mandamus to the next higher court asking that they force the lower court to grant you your divorce. And they will. It really works.

Another example could be the judge or any elected official ruling against you in violation of the law or rules of procedure where you file a writ of mandamus to the next higher court for an order forcing the lower court or other official to obey the law or procedure in a timely manner by ruling in your favor. Yes, it really works and you don't need some greedy lawyer charging you $2,000 to put it together for you. You can do it yourself...and probably better...and definitely quicker.

A writ of prohibition is a law or order that forbids a certain action. It is issued by an appellate court to prevent a lower court from exceeding its jurisdiction or to prevent a nonjudicial officer or entity from exercising a power. For instance, say the judge in your case is the brother of the attorney opposing you and you have asked that this judge recuse himself but he refuses. Now is the time to file a writ of prohibition to the next higher court for removal of said judge. Otherwise, do you have any idea how hard this judge, brother of your opposing attorney, is going to hammer you?

A writ of certiorari is issued by an appellate court, at its discretion, directing a lower court to deliver the record in the case for review. If you feel a lower court decision violated substantive law, constitutional law, or other law, this writ is one avenue of approach for an appeal. You must remember that in any appeal procedure, including writs, you must have a transcript of any previous hearing(s). In a writ of certiorari, the court (or rather the court's law clerks) will peruse your petition for writ of certiorari and transcript to ascertain whether or not the writ should be heard further. If the court concludes that the writ should continue, the court will issue a "Rule To Show Cause" to the other side, appellee, asking for a brief from them as to why the court should not grant you the writ. Procedurally, you will have the opportunity to reply to the appellee's brief. Otherwise, the court will just deny you the writ outright.

Writs are an interesting concept of law and are not to be disregarded lightly. A brief study of this concept might be well worth your time and effort.

SMALL CLAIMS

Small Claims Court is the term usually given to that jurisdiction in the lowest or initial level of the court system whereby folks theoretically are able to comfortably represent themselves. We also know them as Pro Se Litigants, those who represent themselves in a court of law. At this level of the judicial system the rules of civil procedure are generally relaxed considerably, but not disregarded altogether. The courts provide a sort of fill in the blanks pleading document with instructions. There is a monetary limit set for actions in this court. In Florida this amount is $5,000. However, this limit can be as low as $1,750 in Michigan to as high as $15,000 in Tennessee.[74] Lawyers want the limit to be as low as possible since going in excess of this monetary limit by the complaintant requires the implementation of more stringent and complex rules of procedure and thereby necessitate the hiring of an attorney. Certain non-profit, consumer groups like HALT are trying to get the limit raised to $20,000 nationwide. Good Luck! The legal fraternity will never allow it to happen.

The procedures are set up in such a simple manner that most litigants do not have attorneys representing them. Any litigant or party to the action has the right to be represented by an attorney and some do. Even with the theoretically relaxed civil rules of procedure, don't you believe for one minute that the attorney representing the other side won't try to slam dunk the adversary party who does not have an attorney. The attorney will use whatever means at his disposal including

[74] ABA Journal 12/98

but not limited to complex rules of civil procedure. Don't look for sympathy from the judge either. If you don't think that the judge will tend to side with his brethren in the legal fraternity, the lawyer, then you are very naive. You won't be so naive after you've been gutted in the court room by the other party's attorney. Remember, it's a court of law, not a court of justice. Justice doesn't have a damn thing to do with the outcome. If you don't understand that, you will after "your ox has been gored" by the legal fraternity.

If the judge rules against you in small claims court and the other side was represented by an attorney, you can look forward to paying the other side's attorney fees. It's usually up to the discretion of the judge but trust me, the vast majority of the time you are gonna pay. I have seen in many small claim cases where the attorney fees far surpassed the original monetary amount which was in dispute. I specifically recall one small claims case where the attorney fees amounted to $1,800 while the amount in dispute was $200.

Court costs which include the filing fee and cost of process of service are comparatively inexpensive. In my jurisdiction we have a sliding scale filing fee which is dependent on the magnitude of the value or money being sued for. Process of service fees are standard for your area, usually $20-$30 per defendant. When Pro Se Litigants file in my locale they must have two checks, one for the filing fee and one for the local sheriff to cover costs of process of service.

Briefly, I will outline the procedure for small claims filings in my jurisdiction. I would assume a similar procedure would be available in your area.

The first thing I would advise doing before initiating any lawsuit in which you are the plaintiff (the movant or dude doing the suing) is to make damn sure the other party (defendant) has assets or has legal access to assets (money or property) in an amount at least equal to that sum which is in dispute. Nothing will make you feel more stupid than to win your case and the defendant is broke, unemployed, and/or has no assets. The judgment you get you can paste on your wall as wallpaper. But if you don't care about the financial restitution and you just want personal satisfaction in winning, go after him, tiger. Just remember, if the defendant is head of family, you are going to have a hell of a time trying to garnish his wages or bank account. You can record the judgment and it will be a lien on any real property he owns in that county in which it is recorded. Once recorded you can try to perfect the lien if the defendant has any assets. In this connotation perfect means getting your money. Being awarded a judgment is one legal process; perfecting or collecting the judgment is an entirely different legal process. How do you think the attorneys are able to make payments on their castles, airplanes and Jaguars? The legal fraternity takes a simple action and converts it into several complex scenarios. Hello World! Perfecting or collecting on a judgment is a legal process which I will not undertake in this chapter.

When filling in the blanks or putting together your small claims pleading (complaint) make sure you have done your homework before authoring any documents. By doing your homework I mean accumulating any and all documents, data, and other evidence which just might be germane to your action and support your position. You don't have to be a Harvard lawyer to do this, you just need some common sense. If this evidence is filed with the pleading and copies served to the defendant, the defendant will know you are serious and be able to ascertain the strength of your position. After your action is initiated and you need additional evidence or information from an uncooperative defendant you have the discovery process at your disposal to aid you in this endeavor.

Discovery is the legal means available to a party in an action whereby he has access to any documents, data, information, or other evidence of the other party or a third party that is not considered privileged. The theoretical purpose of discovery is to promote justice. Both parties have the legal right to request of each other via interrogatories, admissions and production of documents specified information. Interrogatories are a list of written questions relative to the action which the other party is required to answer in writing. Admissions are a list of written factual statements which one party is asking the other party to admit as to each one being true or not. Production of documents is a request of one party to the other party for copies of certain documents. If the asked party feels the request is out of order, privileged information, or not pertinent to the action at hand, then he may file a Motion for Protection asking the court to deny that particular discovery request of the other party. Better have a good reason for this request, also. If the party asked simply does not answer the discovery request of the asking party, then the asking party can file a Motion to Compel with the court. If you fail to cooperate in the discovery process, you had better have a good excuse for the judge. Be advised, however, the discovery process rarely gets involved in the small claims court process. If you decide to use discovery in your action, I would recommend getting the advice of an independent paralegal or doing some homework at the law library.

Each jurisdiction varies in the number of copies of the complaintant and ancillary attachments to be filed in small claims actions. Most also require stamped, self-addressed envelopes for both plaintiff and defendant. Within six to eight weeks after filing the complaint you should have been notified via mail of a pre-trial hearing. This usually takes place at the court house in front of a judge. In an effort not to waste your time and before going to any court hearing be sure there is documentation in the file affirming that the defendant has been served with the complaint. At the pre-trial hearing the judge will ask if the plaintiff and defendant can resolve this complaint between themselves at this time. There may be a process in your jurisdiction for non-binding mediation at the pre-trial hearing which the judge will tell you to attend right then and there. In my jurisdiction the Court has a dozen or so mediators on hand for the pre-trial hearings. All of these mediators are retirees who took some kind of course from the Court to be mediators in this capacity. None of them are lawyers and they are supposed to help resolve the action in a non-partisan manner. However, it has been my experience that many of them illegally give legal advice in mediation (most of it wrong) and do take sides in an effort to get some kind of agreement with the parties. Personally I think they do more harm than good. Sometimes your action is resolved at this mediation hearing. But remember, the mediation hearing should be non-binding and off the record where whatever is said can not be used at trial. If you don't resolve your action at mediation, go for it and a trial date will be set.

It really doesn't matter how right you are or how wrong you are, how much the law supports you or how much the law is against you, when you walk into that court room. The judge's ruling can go either way. When the law says, "The wall is black" that does not necessarily mean the wall is black. Now don't get me wrong: it definitely should not impugn your position if law and facts support your position. But even then the judge's decision ain't necessarily gonna be a 100% slam dunk in your favor, especially if you are a Pro Se Litigant and the other side is being represented by an attorney.

The casual atmosphere tends to tighten up a little more at the small claims trial. The judge normally will ask the plaintiff to present his side first, then the defendant is heard followed by rebuttal by the plaintiff. If the other side is represented by an attorney, this legal beagle will usually, rudely butt in to speak first and present his side. The judge will probably say nothing and let the attorney proceed. You're a fool if you let this opportunistic attorney take the floor first and you're the plaintiff. Jump up and respectfully ask the judge if courtroom decorum doesn't dictate that the plaintiff presents his case first. If your judge tells you to "sit down, boy", you've got serious problems.

Make sure you have a good presentation of your side of the story. Practice your delivery the night before the trial. Make sure your story flows with a chronological presentation of the facts and evidence. Hearsay, unsubstantiated evidence, is usually not permitted but once again that is up to the discretion of the small claims court trial judge. Hearsay is that verbiage repeated by someone which is not proven with hard evidence. Just because Sally Mae said Lorrie Ann did something does not mean that, in fact, Lorrie Ann did it. However, if you have witnesses that testify accordingly, this evidence is admissible. When the other side makes their presentation take notes. You will have an opportunity to question the other side. Any statement that they made which is not true, you should question them about it. Try to make the other side look questionable to the judge insofar as their creditability is concerned. Bite your tongue and be courteous and humble. Do not call the other side a "lying son-of-a-bitch".

The judge may render a decision then and there or he may decide to mail the parties his decision. If you don't like his decision,

189

you have the right to appeal to the next level of court if you have a transcript of the trial. Don't forget that your right to appeal is a timely one. The appeal period is usually limited to 30 days after the rendition of the judgment. Or you might have the basis for a re-hearing which must be requested in a timely manner, also. I will not go into the basis required for re-hearings here.

UNLICENSED PRACTICE OF LAW

Black's Law Dictionary 7th Edition defines the unlicensed practice of law as "The practice of law by a person, typically a non-lawyer, who has not been licensed or admitted to practice law in a given jurisdiction." This definition continues saying, "The definitions and tests employed by courts to delineate unauthorized practice by non-lawyers have been vague or conclusory, while jurisdictions have differed significantly in describing what constitutes unauthorized practice in particular areas." And "Certain activities, such as the representation of another person in litigation, are generally proscribed. Even in that area, many jurisdictions recognize exceptions for such matters as small claims and landlord-tenant tribunals and certain proceedings in administrative agencies. Moreover, many jurisdictions have authorized law students and others not locally admitted (to the Bar Association) to represent indigent persons or others as part of clinical legal education programs.... Controversy has surrounded many out-of-court activities such as advising on estate planning by bank trust officers, advising on estate planning by insurance agents, stock brokers, or benefit-plan and similar consultants, filling out or providing guidance on forms for property transactions by real estate agents, title companies, and closing-service companies, and selling books or individual forms containing instructions on self-help legal services accompanied by personal, non-lawyer assistance on filling them out in connection with legal procedures such as obtaining a marriage dissolution. The position of Bar Associations has traditionally been that non-lawyer provisions of such services denies the person served the benefit of such legal measures as the attorney-client privilege, the benefits of such extraordinary duties as that of confidentiality of client information and the protection against conflicts of interest, and the protection of such measures as those regulating lawyer trust accounts and requiring lawyers to supervise non-lawyer personnel. Several jurisdictions recognize that many such services can be provided by non-lawyers without significant risk of incompetent service, that actual experience in several states with extensive non-lawyer provision of traditional legal services indicates no significant risk of harm to consumers of such services, that persons in need of legal services may be significantly aided in obtaining assistance at a much lower price than would be entailed by segregating out a portion of a transaction to be handled by a lawyer for a fee, and that many persons can ill afford, and most persons are at least inconvenienced by, the typically higher cost of lawyer services."[75]

The legal fraternity defines the unlicensed practice of law as to what meets the occasion for the definition. If you, as a non-lawyer, were to give me your opinion of the United States Constitution, you would technically be practicing law without a license. If the clerk at the local bank were to return your check to you saying, "Sir, you forgot to endorse your check", she would be practicing law without a license. Yes, these examples do seem ridiculous but no more ridiculous than the convictions by the Courts against paralegals and other non-lawyers for the unlicensed practice of law that have been documented. And they are too numerous to cover in this book.

The USA TODAY[76] published an outstanding editorial headlined "PUBLIC LOSES AS LAWYERS BLOCK ACCESS TO CHEAPER LEGAL HELP". The incident that sparked this editorial was a ruling by a federal judge pursuant to a formal complaint filed by the Texas Bar Association. The Texas Bar complained that a $29.95 nationwide Quicken Family Lawyer computer program which has been available to the public for a goodly number of years was in violation of the state's unlicensed practice of law statute. No one that was not an

---

[75] Restatement (Third of the Law Governing Lawyers Sec. 4 cmt.c (1998)

[76] February 19, 1999

attorney ever complained about this aid and historically, it was responsible for saving folks literally millions of dollars in legal costs. The legal fraternity in Texas could not stand it. The last I heard was that this action was before the Texas Supreme Court. Would you venture a guess as to how the Texas Supreme Court is going to rule...for or against their peers?

The Florida Bar confirms in various membership opinion polls that lawyers do not want any one or anything to possibly even consider jeopardizing their monopoly on their definition of the practice of law. Over 75% of the poll members (Florida lawyers) in the Florida Bar News[77] "believe that legal technicians (paralegals) should **not** be permitted to provide out-of-court legal assistance in routine civil matters." The legal fraternity have become like unto mad dogs in protecting their turf at the expense of the unknowing public. The various State Bar Associations have and are taking thousands of paralegals to court over the pretense of the unlicensed practice of law. Albeit, the vast majority of these independent paralegals are more competent in their respective disciplines than the average attorney in mundane, routine civil matters...and a hell of a lot less expensive and more expedient. I found it interesting to note a recent appellate cite, GEMINI VENTURES OF TAMPA, INC. v. HAMILTON ENGINEERING AND SURVEYING, INC.[78] One of the causes of action in this appeal was the "unlicensed practice of law". The 2nd District Court of Appeals stated the following pursuant to this cause, "We, as part of the legal profession, should be ever vigilant to protect the public from those who seek to provide legal services without the requisite training and knowledge. However, we must also recognize that there are people with experience and expertise capable of providing valuable service to persons involved in legal proceedings without closing the line between legitimate consulting and the unauthorized practice of law. We do a great disservice to the public if we prevent access to the

---

[77] 9/15/99

[78] Florida Law Weekly Vol. 26 D927 April 4, 2001, Florida 2nd DCA

services." This sounds good but you let the State Bar file against a paralegal for the unlicensed practice of law and the kangaroo State Court will unmercifully nail his ass to the bench. There are literally thousands of such cases in the United States but too numerous to detail here. The courts rather have you pay a lawyer $6,000 and take 9 months for a simple step-parent adoption than to pay me $225 and have the mater concluded within 4 weeks.

An independent paralegal friend of mine in south Florida was subjected to an investigation by the Florida Bar 5 years ago under the unlicensed practice of law guise. They were trying to intimidate her into closing down her business. This lady was extremely competent and was providing a great service to the community for the indigent. In fact a number of the local lawyers and judges would send her business. The lawyers kept the clients that they knew they could screw out of significant legal fees for themselves. Anyway, my friend was able to get these lawyers and judges to support her in her defense and the Bar backed off. Last month the Bar started on her again with this unlicensed practice of law crap. They subpoenaed her to a deposition to bring ALL of her clients, documents, data and information for the past 4 years. She phoned me for advice. In light of the results of the last investigation showing her to be squeaky clean, I told her to tell the Bar she had nothing to give them and unless they had some concrete and definitive evidence against her, back off or she would file a complaint against the Florida Bar for malicious prosecution. She did and the Bar backed off.

It is public record that the Florida Bar spends over a million dollars a year on the alleged so-called prosecution of unlicensed practice of law offenders. In Florida hundreds of complaints are filed every year against independent paralegals for the unlicensed practice of law and of these I have seen only one complaint filed by a client while all of the others were filed by lawyers. Does that tell you something? Did I hear someone say, "Greedy bastards"?

As long as there are lawyers and Bar Associations around we will have to contend with the unlicensed practice of law syndrome. It's the nature of the beast.

SHORTS

Michael Doe came to me for help in filing a complaint against a Mr. Smith for not paying a promissory note for $10,000. I put together a Verified Complaint for filing in the County Court since the amount was less than $15,000 but more than $2,500. Doe filed in Brevard County and Smith was served. Smith filed an answer with the Clerk of the Court some 24 days after service or four days past the default time. Pursuant to the Rules of Civil Procedure Mr. Doe could legally file a default because Mr. Smith did not file an answer with the Clerk in a timely fashion. When Doe tried to file a Motion For Default the 23rd day, the Clerk illegally denied him and told him he would have to go to trial. The Clerk would not give Doe the time of day other than to advise him to go hire an attorney. Subsequently, Doe phoned the judge's legal secretary for a hearing. Judge K's legal secretary told Doe that she could not give him a hearing date and that he would either have to hire an attorney or petition the court for a hearing time. Frustrated, Doe phoned me for help. I told him I would get back to him in a few minutes. I then phoned Judge K's legal secretary and told her I needed a hearing date for the Doe vs Smith Case No. 96-xxxxx which would take about 15 minutes. She thought I was a lawyer and was instantly overly cooperative and nice to me. She apologized in telling me that the earliest hearing I could get was 12 days henceforth. I thanked her and assured her the appropriate hearing notices would be mailed out. She thanked me for letting her help me. I then phoned Doe and gave him the hearing date, time and location. The point here, which Doe so aptly stated, is that "the legal fraternity is a tight knit group that really doesn't care or have any empathy for the poor bastard who represents himself."

197

Incidentally, at the final hearing, which was not attended by the defendant, the judge refused to execute the final judgment. She, the judge, said the final judgment document was not properly done and Mr. Doe should hire an attorney to do it.. This final judgment came right out of the Florida Rules of Civil Procedure. I passed it by three lawyers who all said it was proper and they could find nothing wrong with it. I formulated four different final judgments which were presented to the judge in anticipation that she would have to sign one of them. She did.

MCKEE VS DISNEY
Here is another episode about the legal system sticking it to a pro se plaintiff. A Leland McKee, as a pro se litigant, filed a complaint against Disney and lost at the circuit and state district court of appeals level. He then appealed to the 11th District Court of Appeals. Judge G. Kendall Sharp of the 11th District Court of Appeals has never permitted a pro se litigant to present their case in his courtroom. Even though the defendants', Disney and Pepsi, attorneys felt there were merits to at least one of Mr. McKee's counts, Judge Sharp dismissed the complaint nine days before the scheduled trial. Admittedly, both sides had incredible preparation completed by the time the judge dismissed the case. Disney admitted to having spent around $75,000 in this litigation while Mr. McKee, the pro se, spent $112.

JUDGES DO AS THEY PLEASE
Federal law prohibits judges from ruling in cases in which they earlier "expressed an opinion concerning the merits of a particular case in controversy". The law was passed in 1974 in the wake of controversy over the participation by then associate justice William Rehnquist in a 1972 case that resolved an issue on which he had acted as a Justice Department official. "Congress didn't want that kind of thing to happen again," says Hofstra University law professor Monroe Freedman. Nevertheless, United States Supreme Court Justice Clarence Thomas made a ruling in a June 10, 1996 case involving pension benefits of Paul Spink an employee at Lockheed Corp. The case involved interpretation of a law that required Lockheed and other employers to contribute to pension plans of older workers without discriminating on

the basis of age. As chairman of the EEOC in 1988, Justice Thomas argued that the law should not be applied retroactively to benefit older workers who had already been discriminated against. But the IRS disagreed and said companies nationwide should make retroactive payments totaling as much as $3 billion. At a 1988 meeting unrelated to any particular litigation, Thomas said, "We think that substantively, we are absolutely correct." Thomas ruled against retroactively, thereby ratifying his earlier view.

Two legal experts and a lawyer involved in the case say Thomas should have recused himself and not voted, much less written the opinion. "He should not have participated in the case," says New York University law professor Stephen Gillers. "We want to trust that judges are taking their position uninfluenced by an interest in vindicating their prior positions."

Attorney Bert Voorhees who wrote the opinion said he seriously considered filing a motion to ask Thomas to remove himself when the case first went before the court. But he decided not to, fearing he would alienate Thomas and the court. In his brief filed with the court, Voorhees did note Thomas' participation in the issue at the EEOC. "There's no way that the court could have missed the fact that Thomas was involved." said Voorhees.

Thomas did not respond to requests for comment. Steve Smith, a former Thomas law clerk, says, "If it was even a close call, he would have recused."

In the federal judicial system, decisions by justices on whether or not to recuse are reviewed by no other official or body. A federal commission recommended three years ago that the Supreme Court establish some mechanism for reviewing questions about justices' ethics, but the court has not acted.

TAXPAYERS SUBSIDIZE LAWYERS IN EMINENT DOMAIN CASES

Eminent Domain is where a governmental entity takes a person's real property for use in the best interests of the public. Usually these takings are for public roads, easements, and the such. The governmental entity that does the taking compensates the land owner accordingly.   Florida is among the most profligate states in compensating private landowners and their lawyers when taking property for public purposes. Analysts in the early 1990s estimated the system was costing the state (taxpayers) up to $10 million annually in inflated land prices and unnecessary legal fees.

The State of Florida legislature tried in 1984 and again in 1994 to pass reforms aimed at making the attorneys' compensation based on how much they won for their clients.   Previously, the state paid the attorneys mostly on an hourly basis, win or lose.   Scandals erupted because some lawyers were churning hours needlessly, causing the fees in some smaller condemnation cases to far exceed the cost of the land itself.   Many believe the legislature failed in its attempts to curtail this financial smorgasbord for lawyers as evidenced by the fee award in the Panhandle case.

The Panhandle case dates back to the 1980s, when the state decided to acquire some pristine beachfront front in the Panhandle owned by the St. Joe Paper Company. In 1990, St. Joe offered to sell a large portion of it to the state for about $45 million, but the Cabinet rejected that offer. Subsequently, Walton County officials reduced the property's zoning density in order to protect its environmental quality. After the down zoning, which lowered the property's value the State offered St. Joe about $25 million. St. Joe turned this offer down and the case went to court when the State exercised it's right to condemn the property under eminent domain.

A sympathetic local judge sided with St. Joe and rejected the State's condemnation suit. Days later, the State settled with St. Joe for $84 million taxpayers dollars, in an agreement that also allows development of other St. Joe property.

In addition to the $84 million award to St. Joe, the judge awarded a $12 million legal fee to the lawyers who represented St. Joe Paper. This fee, according to the Attorney General of Florida, Bob Butterworth, works out to $4,000 an hour.

This eminent domain scenario is being repeated on a daily basis throughout the State of Florida but usually on a smaller scale. It is just another way in which the legal fraternity ruthlessly sucks taxpayers dollars out of the system for their private benefit.[79]

ALLEGED GENDER DISCRIMINATION - - HOT NEW AREA FOR LAWYERS

Over the past five years, retailers have been terrorized by law firms filing huge gender discrimination suits against chain stores like Florida's Publix and Albertson's. Attorneys were successfully seeking damages against Publix on behalf of women who worked in the chain's administrative offices, bakeries, and other non-retail facilities. Similarly, lawyers were seeking discrimination damages against Albertson's for women employed in its stores. Seeing the success of these actions in the award of unbelievable payments to plaintiffs and unconscionable fees to their attorneys, attorneys are coming out of the woodwork looking for clients to represent in an unprecedented effort to sue retailers. Recently, the firm of Robles & Gonzalez is said to be pursuing a discrimination class-action suit against Pizza Hut on behalf of Hispanic employees.

All of these suits have been based on new changes in state and federal discrimination laws initiated and supported by the legal profession. It has become a financial bonanza for them. Already, the changes in the law have caused potential awards to soar over $100 million in some big class actions. One law firm won $107 million from Lucky Stores, $250 million from State Farm and $29.5 million from Albertson's in recent years. Attorney fees in class actions usually range between 25% and 40% of the total award. Let's see...that's between $97,000,000 and $154,00,000 in legal fees in these cases. Not bad, if I say so myself.

And where do these retailers get the money which they have to pay out in class action suits? In the form of higher prices for goods, insurance, services, etc., which you the consumer pay.

---

[79] Florida Trend Oct. 1996

PETITION FOR MODIFICATION OF CHILD SUPPORT

ES, a divorced mother of two daughters, came to me for help in filing a petition for modification of child support. Her divorce was final in 1991 and she has been receiving the same amount of child support since that time. She came to this country from Poland and her English is not the greatest. Her ex-husband has had some significant salary increases since 1990 and ES thought it was time he contributed more money for the support of his daughters pursuant to Section 61.13, Florida Statutes. The least expensive lawyer she found to aid her in this endeavor wanted $1,500 retainer and more as the case progressed. I charged her a total of $245 for everything. Her final judgment stated that the parties must mediate any changes with reference to the children before applying to the court. I would suppose such changes would include visitation and custody However, child support is a statutorily fixed action that can not be mediated. It is a vested right of the minor children.

We filed a Petition for Modification of Child Support with all required ancillary documents. The husband was served the petition with interrogatories to fill out and return as required by law within 30 days of service. The interrogatories include a financial affidavit to be completed by the husband. The husband refused to submit a financial affidavit, therefore, we filed a Motion to Compel and got a hearing date. Subsequent to this action, the husband's attorney filed a Motion to Dismiss ES's Petition for Modification of Child Support. We had no idea the husband had an attorney. No Notice of Appearance was filed as required by procedure. The attorney certified that he had mailed a copy of his Motion to Dismiss to ES on May 6, 1997 even though it was postmarked May 16th. Attorneys are notorious for lying about the dates of their Certificates of Service. At her hearing on the Motion to Compel on May 21st, Circuit Judge AD lambasted ES because she did not send the original Petition and Motion to Compel to her ex-husband's attorney instead of the ex-husband. ES tried to explain to the judge that (1) she did not know her ex-husband had an attorney, and (2) look at the postmark of May 16th versus the date the attorney certified as May 6th. In other words, even with unrefuted proof that the attorney was a liar. Judge AD told ES to get out of his court and send everything to her ex-husband's attorney again. Now you see what jerks judges can be.

This is another excellent example of a pro se litigant following the Rules of Civil Procedure perfectly, yet having the presiding judge go out of his way to cover the inept attorney of the other side.

PETITION FOR MODIFICATION OF CHILD SUPPORT

RD got his divorce about 8 years ago. He has three children by that marriage. Ordered to pay child support, he was never late in paying and never missed a child support payment. His final judgment decreed that as each child reached the age of eighteen years, graduated from high school, married, died, or was emancipated, that particular child was no longer due child support. What the court and his attorney failed to tell old RD was that for any of this to take effect, it was incumbent upon him to file a petition for modification of child support formally requesting this action; it doesn't happen automatically. The court expects you to hire some greedy attorney for a couple of thousand of dollars or whatever they can squeeze out of you to handle this legal scenario for you. The court continued taking the child support for all three children out of RD's paycheck even though one of the children had reached the age of eighteen years. We charged RD $245 to handle the entire action, regardless of the fact that his ex-wife was very vindictive and would probably fight. Fight what, you may ask! Read further...

We filed the Petition For Modification Of Child Support using all of the forms as authorized by the Florida Supreme Court for pro se litigants. The ex-wife was served by the Sheriff with the petition, summons and request on interrogatories for her financial affidavit. The law states that we could have just mailed the petition to her in this instance but we have our share of fruitcake judges here who take great pride in taking advantage of pro se litigants when they are afforded the least little opportunity. Not wanting to get strung out on the alleged legalities and formalities of service of process, I have found it better to just go ahead and spend the extra $20 in getting someone served rather than arguing with some contrary judge who doesn't know what the hell he's talking about in the first place. RD's ex-wife was served and refused to file her financial affidavit in a timely manner as required by law. She figured that the longer she could hold up this process of RD getting his child support lowered the longer she could milk this poor litigant for additional child support. RD filed a Motion To Compel and Notice of Hearing. At the hearing the judge eagerly wanted to know "who is helping you prepare these documents and what are you being charged?" RD told him the truth as I had prepared him to do so. You see, these judges used to be attorneys. It kills them to see some poor, broke ex-husband handle their own legal affairs, especially in a proper manner, than to mortgage his soul to some incompetent lawyer to handle something as simple, straight forward and mundane as a modification of child support. RD had told me that the least expensive lawyer wanted $1,500 to handle this case with additional fees if it got out of hand. In other words, "Son, I'm gonna suck every penny out of you that I possible can in this endeavor!" The judge signed RD's order to compel his ex-wife to furnish the financial affidavit. She still refused to file her financial affidavit. We prepared a Motion for Contempt for RD on his ex for not obeying the court order compelling her to furnish her financial affidavit as required by law. RD filed the contempt motion and notice of hearing for an 11:00 A.M. Monday, hearing in front of a General Master. The judge just didn't want to waste his valuable time dealing with this as no lawyers were involved. Three days before the hearing, RD gets a thick package in the mail from a lawyer his ex just hired. It contained a Motion To Compel for RD, notice of hearing for 8:30 A.M. that same morning as RD's 11:00 A.M. hearing, a Motion For Contempt against RD and some other minor harassment. RD called me up on Saturday just devastated. He didn't know what to do. I met him at my office and calmly reminded him that the judge would probably rule in favor of the attorney regardless of the fact that the attorney was absolutely and totally wrong pursuant to Florida family law. I told him to try to convince the judge to let him talk for at least two minutes at the hearing. Usually in cases where there is an attorney on one side and a pro se litigant on the other side, the judge lets the lawyer talk but cloisters the pro se litigant. Tell the judge your story in two minutes period. You've approached the court with clean hands, always paid your child support, are using forms the judge himself initiated in this jurisdiction, are doing exactly what the law dictates, and all you want is for your ex-wife to do is obey this judge's order of last month and file her financial affidavit. Telling this to the judge will make it extremely difficult for him to rule in favor of the lawyer. Hope the judge will throw out the rest of this superfluous documentation that the lawyer filed as having no bearing whatsoever in this case. You must remember, the most important thing in the world to this lawyer, above his God if he has one, above his family, above any and everything, is money! The lawyer will do anything for money; there are literally no limits as to what a lawyer will do for money. I see it on a daily basis in my legal business. Incidentally, this lawyer requested that RD pay for this lawyer's legal fees.

RD attended the 8:30 A.M. hearing and followed my advice. Would you believe, the judge ruled in RD's favor.

INVOKE THE RULE

I tell all of my clients that must attend a hearing or meeting in front of a judge or General Master to take as many people with them as possible. They are your witnesses at the hearing if the judge were to do some outlandish thing during the hearing or trial if you haven't hired a court reporter to record everything. It's your constitutional right to be able to appear in court with your friends and/or family. Case law supports this act. This attendance by your friends and/or family tends to get the Court's attention and, therefore, the judge is more conservative about verbally assaulting the pro se litigant in front of him. This is especially true when the other side is represented by an attorney. However, the legal fraternity has found a way around this right of yours. Either side has the right to call any witness to the hearing/trial which they believe will help their cause. Rules of Evidence and law[80] have it that the attorney or judge can request of the court that none of the witnesses be present during the hearing/trial so as not to have the witnesses' testimonial credibility tarnished before they testify. If the witness is present in the courtroom, the attorney can "invoke the rule"

---

[80] Section 90.616, Florida Statutes

which in essence requests the court to order the witnesses to vacate the courtroom until called to testify. Attorneys usually "invoke the rule" when the other side has no attorney and the pro se litigant brought some friends or family (or possibly a media reporter) with them to the hearing. The attorney will tell the judge that he might call as a witness any or all of the friends/family brought to the courtroom by the non-represented pro se litigant and therefore, he, the attorney, "invokes the rule". The judge will gladly order everyone out of the courtroom except for the pro se litigant. Just because the attorney "invoked the rule", it is not mandatory that he call any or all of the individuals ordered out of the courtroom as witnesses. Just another way the judicial fraternity screws the poor pro se litigant.

JUDGES ARE THE SAME!!!

If you missed the November 1, 1998 60 MINUTES program on CBS, you should get a video of it. It is really worth watching. 60 MINUTES played an expose on the Texas Supreme Court justices back in 1987. It showed how the Texas Supreme Court justices were elected by the voters to their positions on the high court bench. Money, being the mother's milk of politics, was needed by these judicial candidates to run a winning campaign. The 60 MINUTES investigation showed how the rulings and decisions by the Texas Supreme Court favored 90% of the time those individuals and special interest groups that financially supported the respective Justices on the Court during their campaigns for election to the high court. This expose by 60 MINUTES back in the late 80's caused such a stir that in the following election, a new group of judges was elected to the Texas Supreme Court. Some 10 years has now passed and you got it! The current Texas Supreme Court is as bad as the previous Texas Supreme Court was 10 years previously. Rulings and decisions by this Court once again run favorable in the vast majority of times to those who contributed financially to the election of these respective judges. Texas is not unique in this endeavor. You are very naive if you don't believe in the old axiom, "Money talks and bullshit walks." If this favoritism occurs on the Supreme Court level, you don't have to be Albert Einstein to ascertain how rampant favoritism runs on the local court levels. And believe me, it does...

WHY DO THE COURTS PUNISH MY KIDS AND ME ???

I can not afford an attorney. My ex-wife has an attorney. My two wonderful girls, ages 6 and 8, are living with me as their mother, my ex-wife, once again is in a drug rehab facility in Orlando, drying out. She pleaded guilty to conspiracy to traffic in illegal drugs (Case No. A97-004113CFF, Seminole County). The Court gave the mother legal custody with me paying court ordered child support to her for the 2 girls. This was back in 1994 when we got our divorce. Since then, the mother has moved repeatedly, been involved with drugs, arrested, and a myriad of other unsavory actions. These actions have all been documented. Read Case No. 93-3767-DR-02-B at the Domestic Relations window of the Seminole County Court House in Sanford. The Court will not grant me legal custody of my two girls and I am supposed to keep paying child support to my ex-wife for these girls even though they are living full time with me. If I stop paying the child support, the Court will send me to jail. Why does the Court punish me and my kids?

The judge in this action historically does not like pro se litigants (folks that can not afford an attorney). He has a reputation of treating pro se people with disdain and contempt. Even though my motions, petitions, answers and other legal jargon are legally correct and many times superior to those of the inept lawyer my ex-wife has, the judge constantly covers for the lawyer and makes me jump through unnecessary legal hoops. Why? Go read the file and see for yourself. Is it because I am not contributing to the financial coffers of the legal fraternity? I wish the entire central Florida citizenry would attend some of my hearings in my endless battle with the Florida legal system to really see what goes on in the troughs of so-called justice. I truly believe the best interests of my daughters are not being served because I can not afford an attorney... And I understand there are thousands of hard working, poor folks just like me that can not afford an attorney. I guess LAW is the bastard child of JUSTICE...

One of my clients in a siege of desperation wrote the above and sent it to the local newspaper editor to print in a possible effort to expedite his case. The newspaper did not print it. I later found out that the CEO and publisher were attorneys. Guess they didn't want to impugn the great reputation of the legal fraternity? Incidentally, since he wrote the above press release, he had a hearing on his Motion To Compell in an effort to get his ex-wife's attorney to produce certain discovery as required by law. The attorney denied ever getting the request from him. My client then produced executed certified mail receipts signed by this lawyer signifying this lawyer was a lying bastard and that he did indeed receive the requests for discovery. The same judge believed the attorney and advised my client he had better hire an attorney for future hearings.

FLA. SCHOOL BOARD SETTLES BUSSING LAWSUIT

The Broward County, Florida school board agreed to pay $485,000 to end a lawsuit filed five years ago that alleged black children were denied the same education as white children. $135,000 was awarded to two black students. It's the first time that black children bussed for desegregation were awarded damages because their rights were violated. The lawyer representing the plaintiff was awarded $350,000 in legal fees![81] Give me a break.

LITIGATION GROWS IN AILING NURSING HOME INDUSTRY

Millions of our elderly citizens, including veterans and widows, require nursing home care in their golden years. Most can not afford paying thousands of dollars a month for this service. Since the recent onslaught of lawsuits by attorneys against nursing homes and the subsequent awards by the courts, costs for nursing homes have exploded. Obviously, these costs must trickle down to the consumer, the elderly needing the services of the nursing home. "Everywhere you

---

[81] USA TODAY 8/3/2000

turn, you're bombarded with law firms chumming for business", says Marty Goetz, administrator for a nursing home. The number of claims against nursing homes nationally has increased 9% each year for the past five years, while the average dollar amount of individual judgments has risen from $64,015 to $112,351, says a study by Aon Worldwide Actuarial Solutions. In Florida, where the trial lawyers got a law passed to make it easier to sue nursing homes, claims jumped 20% each year. Yes siree, lawyers are after the easy money, pandering to baby boomers feeling guilty about putting Mom and Dad in a nursing home.

Having such a large population of elderly, Florida is know as "God's waiting room". and therefore, a disproportionate number of salivating lawyers are ready to sue the nursing homes. The cost of liability insurance policies for nursing homes in Florida and other states is skyrocketing, driven, insurers say, by an increasing number of lawsuits. Many insurers have stopped writing such policies. Others are canceling existing coverage while nursing homes with impeccable records are seeing insurance premiums rising by 75% and more.

And Florida is exporting its lawyers. A handful of attorneys who specialize in suing nursing homes have opened branch offices in Texas, Alabama, Tennessee and other states. Suing nursing homes has become a growth industry for the judicial fraternity.[82]

And guess what? Suing nursing homes has become such a financial success for lawyers that they have recently started law suits against assisted living facilities. According to the Orlando Sentinel,[83] "Florida's assisted-living facilities, created as an option for seniors needing some help but not 24-hour medical care, appear headed for the same crisis as the nursing homes they were designed to relieve." The cycle of high litigation awards and legal fees leading to skyrocketing insurance rates hit the nursing home industry last year and this year the focal point is the assisted living facilities. In the past year dozens of assisted living facilities have been shut down because they could not

---

[82] USA TODAY 6/19/2000

[83] 12/24/2000

afford the state required insurance. Campbell Epes, owner of the 22 bed Xanadu Retirement Residence in Dania Beach, Florida experienced an increase in insurance in one year from $6,500 to $66,000. Somebody has to feed those lawyers, and it is going to be those senior citizens who have to go to the nursing homes and assisted living facilities. Boy, isn't this the pinnacle of capitalism.

This is just another example of milking the financial coffers of the American public by these **Legal Whores.**

LEGAL KITS

Various legal forms and legal kits are being marketed today in a myriad of office supply and discount stores. Legal forms include such documents as quit claim deeds, satisfactions of mortgage, liens, and powers-of attorney. Individually they will cost 35 cents to 75 cents each. Usually legal forms can be purchased in office supply stores or copied from the original in the local law library. Legal kits usually include forms for last will and testaments, divorces, revocable living trusts, incorporations, landlord/tenant evictions as well as a couple of dozen different aspects of law. Legal kits can cost from $6.95 to $29.95. One has to be very cautious in using these forms or kits. Most of them are generic in nature whereas you might require a legal form or kit that is specific to your jurisdiction's idiosyncrasies. If a Pro Se Litigant has to question whether or not he is using a legal form or legal kit correctly, he probably isn't. It's similar to my rational when flying an airplane; "if you have to question whether or not the weather is good enough in which to fly, then it's isn't!"

Improper or incorrect utilization of these forms and kits can end up being extremely more expensive in the long run than initially seeking the services of an independent paralegal or a competent attorney. In an effort to be comfortable in your endeavors regarding certain legal disciplines, once again we recommend a visit to the law library in your area. Usually the librarians will be more than helpful in answering your questions short of giving you what they refer to as legal advice. In addition, certain states such as Florida have publishers that publish inexpensive booklets that are directed to the lay person. One does not have to be a Harvard Law School graduate to understand them. These legal publications discuss such legal disciplines as incorporation, divorce (dissolution of marriage), landlord/tenant eviction, immigration, bankruptcy, traffic violations and many others. They may not direct you specifically through the exact procedural requirements of your jurisdiction, but they surely will help keep you from making a serious blunder in your interpretations and subsequent actions. Believe me, most of these publications and booklets are well worth their cost. If for no other reason, exposure to these publications puts you in a posture to ask more intelligent questions of your independent paralegal or lawyer on the subject matter. Then they are less apt to jerk you around or try to snow you on terminology or overcharge you more than they are going to overcharge you. You may be dumb but you ain't stupid!

CONCLUSION

"I was never ruined but twice: once when I lost a lawsuit, and once when I won one."

VOLTAIRE

Can anything be done to alleviate the financial rape of the country by the legal fraternity? I seriously doubt it. In fact, as I have shown, this cancer has been exported from the United States to other countries around the world quite successfully. Recently, a number of United States law firms opened offices in various foreign venues. Class action litigation and frivolous lawsuits are now starting to be enjoyed by the rest of the world, also. One wonders what the ultimate financial devastation this globalization of the U. S. legal fraternity will have on the world in years to come... I guess we're going to find out.

A number of anecdotes have been suggested to help reverse the legal onslaught in this country. These range from armed insurrection to annihilation of all lawyers and judges to making the judiciary an arm of the legislative section of the government. Of course, none of these recommendations are plausible...I don't think! Hummmmmmmmm... Nevertheless, several possibilities do exist which might be a start to muzzling the awesome power of the judiciary without taking away its real basis for existing, that being to implement equity and justice. I will briefly discuss several here.

I am a strong believer in term limits for ALL elected and appointed officials. Contrary to what opponents say, term limits tend to keep them honest. (What an oxymoron!) They can not build a dynasty and be so unapproachable to the public. These same principles would apply to judges, both local and federal. And lifetime appointments to the federal bench are a travesty of justice. No one, absolutely no one can justify appointing a person to public office for life. Even the United States Supreme Court should be held accountable for some of the asinine decisions they express. Hold them accountable to the public as the voters of Florida do: the District Court of Appeals and State Supreme Court justices are voted on every four years. The justices do not have opponents on the ballot but they must receive 50%+ of the cast vote to retain their positions on the bench. Otherwise, they are removed from the bench and the Governor must replace them with another appointee. It's not perfect but it works and is effective. In fact, the next election in Florida has generated some significant moneys and interest in replacing the present Florida Supreme Court for their debacle concerning the last presidential election between Messrs. Bush and Gore. Two large, well financed political action committees have been registered with the Florida Division of Elections for this purpose. Should be interesting. Appointed District Court of Appeal judges are just as vulnerable. In Florida, circuit and county judges are up for re-election every 6 and 4 years, respectively.

Legislative reform is another way to harness the unlimited power of the legal fraternity. However, this tends to be difficult because a large number of our legislators from the local to the federal levels are attorneys themselves. It's kind of like the fox guarding the chicken coop. Plus the fact that the vast majority of legislators that are not attorneys are afraid of the organized lawyer organizations which could oppose their respective re-elections. Remember, an elected official's primary concern is not his God or his family or his constituents; it is getting re-elected at whatever the cost. In spite of all of this, the State of Texas under the auspices of public outcry and demand recently legislated certain judicial reforms. It can be done.

The Citizens for a Sound Economy (PAC) commissioned the Perryman Group, an economic research and analysis group based in Waco, Texas to quantify and evaluate the impact of the recent legal reforms implemented by the Texas legislature. A complete report of this study is available from the Citizens for a Sound Economy (1250 H Street, NW, Suite 700, Washington, D.C.20005, phone 1-888-564-6273). Basically, the result of this report has been a more efficient and effective use of the state's scarce economic resources, savings on the goods and services purchased by consumers, and a stimulus to economic development. These efforts have benefited the entire state. I would like to take the liberty here of quoting the report. "The results of the analysis reveal that the total cost of the (legal) tort system in Texas in 2000 was $15.482 Billion. In the absence of recent (legislative) changes, the cost would have been $25.889 Billion. The total direct savings were, thus, $10.407 Billion.... Savings to the typical Texas household in terms of lower prices and total personal income may be viewed as equivalent to a $1,078 annual reduction in the (legal) tort tax." Texas still has a long way to go but this is a start and an excellent example of what can be done to hold the onslaught of the legal fraternity in check. The entire report is well worth getting and perusing in its entirety.

DO NOT elect lawyers to any public office! Keep them out of positions of power as much as possible. I will not belabor these statements as they are self-explanatory. Use a little common sense. Re-elect incumbent judges only under certain criteria. Never return a judge to the bench more than once. Don't be responsible for helping create an insensitive dynasty in the courthouse.

Don't push your child to attend law school, unless of course, the primary rational is strictly for the money. This country is inundated with attorneys trying to generate more novel ways to litigate. We really don't need any more lawyers. Let attrition diminish the supply back to an acceptable level.

Organize and picket for judicial justice at the local level. Form groups to meet at the public library or local school or some other convenient public location. Picket the court house, say, the second Wednesday of every month in the interests of justice. Share your legal horror stories. Get the media involved. The legal fraternity hates nothing more than to have a story publicized telling of how some lawyer or judge literally or figuratively screwed some poor citizen. Keep the heat on the legal fraternity!

I seriously doubt that whatever means are used to castigate the legal fraternity will have little effect in having the pendulum change course and swing toward the right, more conservative station. However,

I do believe the pressure exerted by common citizens will help stymie the continued advancement of this legal cancer.

If you become a victim of this legal process and get caught up in the quicksand of legal monetary greed, be cool. Take stock of your position and use a little common sense. You have plenty of company. Hang in there and God bless you.

AUTHOR BIOGRAPHY

The author was born in Brooklyn, New York in the late 1930's. The family matriculated to Chicago when he was about 7 years old via a several year sojourn in Mississippi. His father was from Madison, Alabama and his mother from Champaign, Illinois. His father literally worked himself to death at the age of 44 years. In fact both of his parents died at the age of 44 years. The author ended up in a Chicago orphanage while his only sister (no brothers) went to an aunt's care in Springfield, Illinois. The orphanage was just two blocks from skid row in Chicago. The stay at the orphanage was real culture shock and a learning experience for the author. At the age of ten, he ran away from the Chicago orphanage to his father's sister farm in Mississippi. This aunt treated him as one of her own. Following graduation from high school, the author attended college in Mississippi for two years and then joined the United States Marine Corps. Boot camp at Paris Island, South Carolina had a very profound effect on this young man. His tour in the Marine Corps included such diversity as the Marine Corps Rifle Team, embassy duty, fleet recon, Viet Nam, Burma, Thailand, and the Philippines. After three years of military duty, he returned to college in Mississippi where he graduated with a degree in chemistry and subsequently, with his wife and new born son, began employment as a bench chemist in New Jersey with a large oil company. His next job was technical sales for a large corporation which entailed technical sales covering the southeast United States. This lasted for some 6 years of constant traveling. The author and his family finally ended up residing in central Florida in the latter 1960's or before Disney World. He left the chemistry discipline and his new vocations became real estate and

217

politics. He became successful in both endeavors. So much so, that he and several of his cohorts were indicted by the local grand jury on alleged election law violations in the mid-seventies. At the same time a recession hit the country and he went broke. Instead of declaring bankruptcy, he worked three jobs in order to honor all of his debts which he successfully paid off within 4 years. Continuing his ventures in real estate and politics, he was now well seasoned and a hell of a lot smarter. He had numerous positions both corporate and eleemosynary in the community including President and Founder of the Association of Florida Bass Clubs and the Florida Bass Fisherman magazine, President of United Cerebral Palsy, Chairman of the Port Authority (appointed by the Governor), airplane pilot (instrument rated). Two months after his son graduated from medical school, the author was amicably divorced from his wife of 27 years. His dissolution of marriage action and the previous indictment by the grand jury were instrumental in his entering the legal discipline. The author earned a degree in legal studies and opened up his own legal clinic. It is the experiences he witnessed within the legal community that generated his strong drive to write this book.

The author is a member of the American Bar Association.

Index

The Bosphorus Corporation
P. O. Box 180292
Casselberry, Florida 32718-0292
Facsimile 407-327-8444
Email tbinford@cfl.rr.com

ISBN 155369672-7

9 781553 696728